African American Recipients
of the Medal of Honor

African American Recipients of the Medal of Honor

*A Biographical Dictionary,
Civil War through Vietnam War*

CHARLES W. HANNA

McFarland & Company, Inc., Publishers
Jefferson, North Carolina, and London

Library of Congress Cataloguing-in-Publication Data

Hanna, Charles W.
African American recipients of the Medal of Honor : a biographical
dictionary, Civil War through Vietnam War / by Charles W. Hanna.
p.   cm.
Includes bibliographical references and index.

ISBN 0-7864-1355-7 (illustrated case binding : 50# alkaline paper)

1. Medal of Honor — Biography — Dictionaries.   2. African American
soldiers — Biography — Dictionaries.   3. United States — Armed
Forces — Biography — Dictionaries.   I. Title.
UB433.H35   2002
355.1'342 — dc21   2002006974

British Library cataloguing data are available

On the cover: Sergeant Christian Fleetwood, USA.
Background ©2002 Photospin.

Manufactured in the United States of America

McFarland & Company, Inc., Publishers
Box 611, Jefferson, North Carolina 28640
www.mcfarlandpub.com

Acknowledgments

I am indebted to the members of the Medal of Honor Historical Society. This is a group of individuals, historians, and scholars who all share a special interest in the history of the Medal of Honor and its recipients. Working with these individuals has been an absolute pleasure. I need to mention by name Preston Amos and Ray Collins who have spent countless hours researching the history of recipients of the Medal of Honor. Preston Amos has particularly specialized in African American recipients of the Medal of Honor and the information he contributed to my research and to this book has been invaluable. I also acknowledge my debt to Edward F. Murphy, the president of the Medal of Honor Society, who has been a key individual in creating and maintaining my own interest in Medal of Honor research.

I am also greatly indebted to Kae Loy Hanna, who has spent countless hours proofreading and editing my manuscripts. Her service has been very valuable to me, and her support has made this book possible.

The photographs contained in this book were obtained from, and are used with the permission of, the U.S. Army Military History Institute located in Carlisle Barracks, Pennsylvania. Their assistance and cooperation in providing me with the photographs is also greatly appreciated.

Finally, I would like to acknowledge the recipients of the Medal of Honor, all of whom are my personal heroes. My study of their lives has turned into a passion. I am constantly amazed at the courage of these men whose stories have so greatly enriched my own life.

Table of Contents

Chapter 2—The Indian Wars (1866–1890)   55

Chapter 3—Peacetime from 1872 to 1890   99

Chapter 4—The Spanish-American War (1898)   107

Chapter 5—World War I (1914–1918)   119

Chapter 6—World War II (1941–1945)   123

Chapter 7—The Korean War (1950–1953)   137

Chapter 8—The Vietnam War (1960–1975)   145

Introduction:
History of the Medal
of Honor

The Medal of Honor is one of the world's most highly respected military awards. The Medal of Honor was first authorized by Congress during the Civil War, on December 21, 1861. Since that time, there have been 3,457 men and one woman who have earned this prestigious award.

The Medal of Honor is a recognition of courage in a stressful, life-threatening situation. It is awarded for showing leadership when it is needed the most. It represents the willingness to place oneself in harm's way to save the life of another. Most of all, the medal represents valor at its highest level, above and beyond the call of duty.

Taking up a fallen flag when all the enemy guns are focused on those colors and the man carrying them, as Christian Fleetwood did; diving into a raging sea to effect the rescue of a drowning comrade, as Daniel Atkins did; facing certain death by throwing oneself onto a live grenade so that your buddies will live, as Milton L. Olive did; and charging an enemy position when the chance of survival is practically nonexistent, as Edward Radcliff did, are all examples of medal-worthy heroics.

In the Revolutionary War, Americans struggled to free themselves from the tyranny of Europe, and it became popular in America to disdain all things European. Medals for bravery were among those things disdained. The image of the European general, with medals all over his uniform, was not one that Americans wished to copy. The U.S.

1

military was made up of citizen soldiers, all of whom were just doing their duty.

The first formal system for rewarding acts of individual gallantry by the nation's fighting men was established by General George Washington on August 7, 1782. Designed to recognize "any singularly meritorious action," the award consisted of a purple cloth heart. Because of America's disdain for decorations, records show that only three persons ever received the award: Sergeant Elijah Churchill, Sergeant William Brown, and Sergeant Daniel Bissel, Jr.

The Badge of Military Merit, as it was called, fell into oblivion until 1932, when General Douglas MacArthur, then Army Chief of Staff, pressed for its revival. Officially reinstituted on February 22, 1932, the now familiar "Purple Heart" was at first an Army award, given to those who had been wounded in World War I or who possessed a Meritorious Service Citation Certificate. In 1943, the order was amended to include personnel of the Navy, Marine Corps, and Coast Guard. Coverage was eventually extended to include all services and "any civilian national" wounded while serving with the Armed Forces.

Although the Badge of Military Merit fell into disuse after the Revolutionary War, the idea of a decoration for individual gallantry remained through the early 1800s. In 1847, after the outbreak of the Mexican-American War, a "Certificate of Merit" was established for any soldier who distinguished himself in action, although no medal went with the honor. After the Mexican-American War, the award was discontinued, which meant there was no military award with which to recognize the nation's fighting men.

Early in the Civil War, a medal for individual valor beyond the call of duty was proposed to general-in-chief of the Army Winfield Scott. General Scott, however, was from the old school and still felt medals smacked of European affectation, and he killed the idea.

The idea of a medal for courage above and beyond the call of duty found support in the Navy, however, where it was felt that recognition of courageous acts in strife was needed. Public Resolution 82, containing a provision for a Navy medal of valor, was signed into law by President Abraham Lincoln on December 21, 1861. The medal was "to be bestowed upon such petty officers, seamen, landsmen, and Marines as shall most distinguish themselves by their gallantry and other seamanlike qualities during the present war."

Shortly after this, a resolution similar in wording was introduced on behalf of the Army. Signed into law July 12, 1862, the measure provided for awarding a Medal of Honor "to such noncommissioned officers and privates as shall most distinguish themselves by their gallantry in action, and other soldier-like qualities, during the present insurrection." Although it was created for the Civil War, Congress made the Medal of Honor a permanent decoration in 1863.

The first deed of valor for which a Medal of Honor was awarded was performed by Private Francis Brownell on May 24, 1861, more than a year before the Army Medal of Honor had been approved by Congress. Private Brownell attacked and killed a Rebel, who had shot and killed Brownell's commanding officer, E. Elmer Elsworth, the colonel of the 11th New York Volunteer Infantry.

The first sailor to earn the Medal of Honor was Captain of the Top John Williams of the U.S.S. *Pawnee.* During the attack on Mathias Point, Virginia, on June 21, 1861, Williams, although severely wounded in the thigh by a musket ball, retained command of his assault boat. When the flagstaff was shot away, he held the stump of it that still secured the flag in his hand and rallied his men.

Corporal John Mackie was the first U.S. Marine to earn the Medal of Honor. On May 15, 1862, aboard the U.S.S. *Galena,* Corporal Mackie was involved in the attack on Fort Darling on the James River in Virginia. Ignoring the heavy volume of enemy fire being directed on the ship, Mackie maintained his position on the deck, firing at the rifle pits on shore. When ordered to man one of the *Galena's* guns because several members of the gun crew had been killed or wounded, Corporal Mackie manned the weapon with both skill and courage.

Sergeant William H. Carney of the famous 54th Massachusetts was the first African American to earn the Army's Medal of Honor, and Contraband Robert Blake was the first African American to earn the Navy Medal of Honor. Both men earned their awards during the Civil War. Private First Class James Anderson, Jr., was the first African American in the U.S. Marine Corps to earn the Medal of Honor; he earned the medal in Vietnam.

Black Americans have served in every one of America's conflicts since the Revolutionary War. Since the Medal of Honor's inception 88 African Americans have earned the distinction: Civil War — Army 18, Navy 8; Indian Wars — Army 18; Peacetime, 1872–1890 — Navy 8; Spanish-American War — Army 5, Navy 1; World War I — Army 1; World War II — Army 7; Korean War — Army 2; Vietnam War — Army 15, Marine Corps 5; Totals — Army 66, Navy 17, Marine Corps 5.

The recipients of the Medal of Honor are true American heroes.

They include a conscientious objector who, when his patrol was pinned down in World War I, moved forward on his own to clear out the Germans. When he came back down the hill, he was escorting 132 German prisoners. When asked how he had accomplished this feat, he responded that he had "just sort of surrounded them." A Marine pilot in World War II took his squadron of 24 fighters over a Japanese fighter base and over the radio insulted the Japanese pilots and dared them to come up to fight. When 60 Japanese fighters answered his challenge the Marines shot down 20 of them without the loss of a single plane. Also during World War II, there was a soldier who, because of his religious beliefs, would not use a weapon; but on Okinawa when his division was forced off of a hill in a fierce Japanese counter attack, he stayed on the hill alone and rescued 75 of his wounded comrades.

The recipients of the Medal of Honor are representative of the diversity of the American people. Whites, African Americans, Hispanics, Orientals and Native Americans have all earned the medal. They are made up of homegrown Americans as well as new immigrants fighting for their new country. They include Catholics, Protestants, Mormons, Seventh-Day Adventists, Jews and Free Masons.

In recent years, the Medal of Honor has become known as the medal a person must die to receive. In fact, during the Korean War, over 70 percent of the medals awarded were posthumous.

Among military people, the Medal of Honor and its recipients are held in the highest reverence. General George Armstrong Custer once offered to exchange all his rank and gold braid for a Medal of Honor; General George Patton said he would give his immortal soul for such an award; and President Harry Truman, as he hung the medal around the neck of one Medal of Honor recipient, said he would rather have the Medal of Honor than be president. None of these men were so honored.

Several years ago, at a party in the South, a soldier climbed up on the shoulders of one of his comrades, trying to get a balloon that had gotten loose and now dangled from the ceiling. As the soldier made a grab for the string tied to the balloon, he lost his balance and went tumbling to the floor at the feet of a lieutenant colonel, who was not amused. "What are you trying to do," demanded the officer, "earn a Medal of Honor?" "Oh no sir," replied the soldier. "I've got that; I was just trying to snag a balloon for one of the kids." In a second, the officer saw the blue-flecked ribbon over the breast pocket of the young man's uniform, mumbled an embarrassed apology and beat a hasty retreat.

On another occasion, a group of officers at the Pentagon were preparing to meet Audie Murphy, who, at the time, was a Hollywood actor. Murphy had earned the Medal of Honor in World War II. A colonel and a brigadier general were debating whether it was appropriate to salute the man who had only been a second lieutenant. The colonel stated that he could find nothing in the regulations about saluting a Medal of Honor recipient. "Well," exclaimed the general, "I don't give a hoot what you say. He's a Medal of Honor man and by the Gods, he rates a salute in my book."

It does in my book, too. Here is my salute to the African American soldiers, sailors and Marines who have earned the highest award this country has to give for valor — the Medal of Honor.

Chapter 1

The Civil War (1861–1865)

At the beginning of the Civil War, there was a widespread belief that blacks were an inferior race and that black men would not, or could not, fight. Most Federal authorities were willing to employ ex-slaves ("contrabands") as laborers with the Union Army but there was widespread opposition to their being utilized as soldiers. A corporal in the 74th New York voiced the general sentiment when he stated, "We don't want to fight side by side with the nigger. We think we are a too superior race for that."

General William T. Sherman felt that it was "unjust to the brave soldiers and volunteers" to place them on an equal basis with blacks. He added, "I cannot bring myself to trust Negroes with arms in positions of danger and trust."

There were also a great host of abolitionists and humanitarians who saw compelling reasons that black men should be given the opportunity to fight for the freedom of their race. Black soldiers would strengthen Federal armies and, at the same time, would sap the Confederacy of its manpower potential. Further, black soldiers would earn for themselves, and for their race, the right to participate in American democracy. As the ex-slave Frederick Douglass stated:

> Once let the black man get upon his person the brass letters, U.S., let him get an eagle on his button, and a musket on his shoulder and bullets in his pocket, and there is no power on earth which can deny that he has earned the right to citizenship in the United States.

Three premature attempts were made in early 1862 to organize black units. Two of these attempts met with bitter disappointment. The first occurred in the Department of the South which was the grandiose name given to Federal toeholds in South Carolina, Georgia and Florida. General Dave Hunter, the 60-year-old commander of the Department of the South, issued an unauthorized emancipation proclamation. Then, on the first anniversary of the firing on Fort Sumner, General Hunter (now nicknamed "Black Dave") began recruiting ex-slaves for a regiment, the 1st South Carolina. Congress, however, refused to recognize the regiment, and no pay nor equipment were issued to the black soldiers. After four months of frustration, General Hunter gave up on his project and the 1st South Carolina was disbanded. Charles Francis Adams, Jr., of the 1st Massachusetts Cavalry, wrote his father on August 10, 1862, from Hilton Head, South Carolina: "General Hunter's Negro regiment was disbanded yesterday.... Its breaking up was hailed here with great joy, for our troops have become more anti–Negro than I could have imagined."

At the same time, General James H. Lane organized the 1st Kansas Colored Volunteers. General Lane ignored the warnings of Secretary of War Edwin Stanton that organizing black units would only lead to trouble. General Lane sent the 1st Kansas Colored Volunteers out on scouting missions and allowed them to engage Confederate guerrillas in a number of minor actions. It was not until well into 1863 that the Federal Government accepted the 1st Kansas Colored Volunteers into service. By then, its seasoned veterans resented being designated as recruits.

The first black regiment to become an official component of the U.S. Army was organized by General Benjamin F. Butler. General Butler himself had a very negative opinion concerning the qualifications of blacks as soldiers. "By long habit and training," the General wrote "[the Negro has] acquired a great horror of fire-arms, sometimes ludicrous in the extreme when the weapon is in his hand."

Nevertheless, one of Butler's brigadiers was a Vermont abolitionist named James W. Phelps. General Phelps began organizing 300 contrabands for what he hoped would become three regiments. General Butler opposed the project. "Phelps has gone crazy," Butler wrote. "He is as mad as a March Hare on the nigger question." The animosity between the two generals soon led to Phelps' resignation. But once Phelps was out of the way, General Butler began to organize three black regiments himself. Commenting on General Butler's reversal one Federal official wrote that "General Phelps had the start on him, while Gen. B.

wanted the credit of doing the thing himself, and in his own way. And he is doing it, shrewdly and completely, as he does everything."

General Butler's new regiments were designated the 1st, 2nd, and 3rd Regiments, Louisiana Native Guards. According to General Butler, all of the recruits in his new regiments were freedmen and he thereby avoided the thorny issue of arming slaves. No one, however, ever inquired of the blacks enlisting in the new regiments if they were or had been slaves. It was kind of a Civil War "don't ask, don't tell" policy.

The first major offensive launched by black soldiers occurred on May 27, 1863, at Port Hudson, Louisiana. Some 1,080 members of the 1st and 3rd Louisiana Native Guards formed the right of the Federal assaulting force against the 6,000-man Confederate garrison. The black soldiers were assigned to attack one of the strongest natural positions along the Mississippi River. The attack was repulsed by the Rebels, but even in defeat, the conduct of the black soldiers was admirable to all. The black units suffered 37 killed, 155 wounded and 116 missing. One of the casualties was Color Sergeant Anselmas Planciacois of the 1st Louisiana. That morning he had received the colors from his colonel with the statement: "Colonel, I will bring back the colors with honor or report to God the reason why." Sergeant Planciacois was mortally wounded in the assault. He was observed by one reporter as having hugged the colors to his breast as he fell.

On July 18, 1863, the 54th Massachusetts, commanded by the 25-year-old Colonel Robert Gould Shaw, participated in the attack on Fort Wagner. The men of the 54th had not had food or sleep for two days, but they did not falter in leading the charge across three quarters of a mile of open sand towards Fort Wagner. The hand to hand fighting was vicious. The 54th momentarily gained a foothold in the fort, but was then pushed back. Colonel Shaw and three other officers were killed in the assault. Eleven officers and 135 men were wounded. Another 100 men were missing in action and presumed dead.

In 1863, black soldiers fought well. They behaved well and fought credibly, for both the Union and themselves. As black regiments were raised and tested in battle, like the famous 54th Massachusetts at Fort Wagner, the tide of opinion began to turn in favor of the black troops. Most notably some of the opinions of the senior Union officers concerning the value of black soldiers began to change. In August 1863, General U.S. Grant wrote to President Abraham Lincoln:

> By arming the Negro we have added a powerful ally. They
> make good soldiers and taking them from the enemy weakens

> him in the same proportion they strengthen us. I am most
> decidedly in favor of pushing this policy.

During their three years' service in the Civil War, black soldiers participated in at least 39 major battles and 410 minor engagements.

A total of 178,895 African Americans served as Federal soldiers during the Civil War. They were organized into 120 infantry regiments, 12 heavy artillery regiments, 10 light artillery batteries and seven cavalry regiments. African Americans made up a total of 12 percent of the entire Federal armies, and 134,111 black soldiers came from slave holding states.

African American soldiers faced a number of difficulties in serving their country and fighting to free their brothers and sisters. They were paid just $7 per month pay and $3 per month for clothing, while white soldiers received $13 per month pay and $3.50 for clothing. When some of the black soldiers stood up against this inequality, they were arrested and tried for mutiny. Sergeant William Walker of the 3rd South Carolina was charged with mutiny and executed by the U.S. Army for leading a strike over the issue of equal pay. The disparity in wages was not corrected by Congress until June of 1864.

White officers generally assigned black regiments a great portion of the manual labor tasks which soldiers had to perform. This increased a sense that black soldiers could not fight and were good only for manual labor.

If they were captured, black soldiers were subject to being executed by their Southern captors. This threat caused President Lincoln to try to keep them in areas where their chance of being captured was minimal but this also kept black units out of the fighting. Finally, President Lincoln had to threaten the South with retaliation if black Union soldiers were executed.

In battle, the Confederates were especially tough on black soldiers. On April 12, 1864, at Fort Pillow, Tennessee, at least 200 black soldiers were massacred by Confederate forces under the command of Nathan Bedford Forrest. The next week at Poison Spring, Arkansas, captured and wounded black soldiers were killed by the victorious Rebels.

On April 25, 1864, at the battle of Mark's Mill, Arkansas, the Rebels again gave no quarter to the defeated black troops. John N. Edwards of Confederate Jo Shelby's division stated: "The battlefield was sickening to behold. No orders, threats, or commands could restrain the men from vengeance on the Negroes...."

Early in the war, the Confederacy was unwilling to exchange captured black soldiers on a man for man basis, as to do so would be to admit their equality. By the time the Confederate government was willing to exchange their black prisoners on a man for man basis, the Union had adopted a no exchange policy to deny the South of manpower.

The War Department had a policy against granting commissions to black soldiers. Notwithstanding this policy, about 75 to 100 African Americans were commissioned as officers. The highest was that of a lieutenant-colonel.

About 29,000 African Americans served in the Union Navy, which was an integrated service. None of the African Americans made the rank of officer.

Despite all of the disadvantages, dangers and hardships, African Americans served their country with honor during the Civil War. Eighteen African American soldiers and seven African American sailors earned the Medal of Honor. The stories of their bravery, valor and self sacrifice follow.

Landsman Aaron Anderson, USN

U.S.S. Wyandank

Aaron Anderson was born in 1811 on a farm in Plymouth, North Carolina. As a young man, Anderson moved to Philadelphia, Pennsylvania, where he worked as a cook. On April 17, 1863, the 52-year-old Anderson enlisted as a Landsman in the Navy at Philadelphia, Pennsylvania. When Anderson signed on to the U.S.S. Wyandank, his name was erroneously entered on the ship's logs as Sanderson and his Medal of Honor was issued under the name of Aaron Sanderson.

On March 17, 1865, Landsman Anderson was on an expedition to clear Mattox Creek, Virginia, of Rebels. By the last year of the war, smuggling was the South's only means of securing outside supplies and munitions. The Rebels used the creeks and streams that flowed into the Potomac as hiding places for their desperate smuggling activities. The Potomac River Flotilla waged a daily war against the smugglers and the guerrilla forces of Major John Mosby.

A small howitzer launch had been disembarked from the U.S.S. Don and was making its way up Mattox Creek, one of the hundreds of creeks that emptied into the Potomac in that area. The launch was under the command of Ensign Summers, who sat in the stern and manned the rudder. Boatswain Patrick Mullen was assigned to operate the small howitzer. The remainder of the crew consisted of a number of Landsmen, all of whom were black, and manned the oars. Landsman Aaron Anderson was one of these. The launch moved slowly and silently up the right fork of the Mattox Creek, while 70 men marched along the bank for support. From some underbrush, several snipers opened fire on the land force. Ensign Summers brought the launch around and Boatswain Mullens prepared to fire the howitzer, but the Rebels had all fled before he could pick a target.

Farther up the creek, the launch found four small boats, which the Rebels had abandoned. The land force was waived to the spot and the boats were destroyed. While the land force was busy destroying the boats, Ensign Summers turned the launch around and went back down the creek to the last fork. A signal from the bridge of the *Don* ordered the launch up the left fork of Mattox Creek. Without the support troops on the land, the assignment became much more dangerous. Ensign Summers noted that the water in the left fork was deeper, which meant that the launch might encounter one or more larger craft, which could be armed with guns much larger than Mullen's howitzer. In addition, moving up the creek without the land force increased the exposure of those in the launch to an attack from the shore. Everyone became a little more tense as Anderson and his fellow landsmen pulled on their oars and the launch moved up the creek.

For a time all was quiet. Then the launch came around a bend in the creek, and the creek widened out into a small lakelike area. Three schooners lay anchored just ahead, along piers on the left bank. Ensign Summers guided the launch alongside the schooners and Boatswain Mullens aimed the howitzer at the nearest schooner. All three boats, however, appeared to be deserted.

Within 50 yards of the nearest schooner, a single musket shot cracked out from the underbrush on the left bank, followed immediately by a volley from about 400 muskets. Several slugs ripped through the gunwales of the launch. Mullen fired his howitzer and a flame shot up from the underbrush, throwing the body of one unfortunate Rebel high into the air.

"Row!" Summers commanded. Anderson and the other Landsmen pulled on their oars and under heavy fire got the launch moving towards the schooners. The Rebels had been caught unprepared and the schooners were unmanned. This was a good thing as one well-placed shot from one of the cannons would have ended the expedition in a hurry. Boatswain Mullen dug three fire-bombs from the ready box and, standing in the launch completely exposed to the enemy fire, hurled one onto the first of the schooners. Ensign Summers positioned the launch so that the schooners momentarily protected them from the fire from the shore and Mullen threw fire-bombs onto the two other schooners. Soon all three ships were ablaze.

Ensign Summers reversed course and the launch started back down stream. As soon as the launch cleared the schooners, the Rebel fire directed against them recommenced and was heavier than ever. It was as if the Rebels, angered by the loss of their boats, were now determined that the sailors were going to pay in blood for what they had done. So intense was the fire from the shore that half of the oars were cut away and the gunwales of the launch were pierced in several places. Ensign Summers attempted to respond to the enemy fire, but had the barrel of the musket he was using shot away while he was in the process.

Boatswain Mullen used the powder flash from the muskets as a target and returned fire with the howitzer as rapidly as possible. Anderson and those Landsmen who still had oars were pulling for all they were worth as the launch pulled away from the murderous fire. Those Landsman whose oars had been shot away were barely able to keep the launch afloat by bailing the water that was pouring in from the bullet holes.

Once the launch was well out of range, it was time to assess the damage and the casualties. The small launch had been almost shot to pieces. But notwithstanding all the lead that fired at the launch, only one of the Landsmen had been slightly wounded.

Landsman Aaron Anderson and Boatswain Patrick Mullen were singled out by Ensign Summer for their coolness and courage under fire. Landsman Anderson's Medal of Honor citation reads as follows:

> Served on board the U.S.S. *Wyandank* during a boat expedition up Mattox Creek, March 17, 1865. Participating with a boat crew in the clearing of Mattox Creek, Anderson carried out his duties courageously in the face of a devastating fire, which cut away half the oars, pierced the launch in many places and cut the barrel of a musket being fired at the enemy.

After his term of service in the Navy, Aaron Anderson disappeared from history and nothing further is known about his life.

Private Bruce Anderson, USA

142nd New York Infantry

Bruce Anderson was born on June 19, 1845, at Mexico City, Mexico. Anderson was a farmer in New York when the war began. On August 31, 1864, Anderson enlisted at Schenectady, New York, in Company K, 142nd New York Infantry.

Private Anderson earned the Medal of Honor on January 15, 1865, at Fort Fisher, North Carolina. Volunteers were requested to move ahead of the main attacking columns and cut down the palisading so that the following soldiers could enter the fort unhindered.

Private Anderson was among the thirteen men who volunteered for this hazardous duty. Under an intense fire from the defenders of the fort, Private Anderson and the others coolly set about their work of cutting down the palisade. In a letter dated January 16, 1865, General Adelbert Ames listed the names of the thirteen men who had volunteered to cut down the palisading and recommended that each man be awarded a medal. The letter was misplaced and the medals were not issued.

After the war, Anderson lived in Illinois and eventually settled in Amsterdam, New York. In 1914, Anderson hired an attorney seeking to be awarded a Medal of Honor for his actions at Fort Fisher. At Anderson's request, the Adjutant General of the Army conducted an investigation and General Ames' letter was found. The Adjutant General issued a Medal of Honor to Anderson on November 18, 1914.

The Adjutant General determined that only one man on General Ames' list, Private Zachariah C. Neahr, had been awarded a medal. Neahr's medal had been issued on September 11, 1890, after he had made a request. Further investigation showed that three other men on General Ames' list, George Merrill, Alaric B. Chapin and Dewitt C. Hotchkiss, were still alive. It was recommended that they be awarded medals as well.

Medals were issued to Merrill and Chapin. Somehow, Hotchkiss got overlooked again and never received a medal.

Bruce Anderson died on August 22, 1922, at St. Peter's Hospital, in Albany, New York. He is buried in the Green Hill Cemetery, Amsterdam, New York.

Private William H. Barnes, USA

38th U.S. Colored Troops

William Henry Barnes was born in 1845 at St. Mary's County, Maryland. On February 11, 1864, Barnes enlisted as a private in Company C, 38th U.S. Colored Troops at Norfolk, Norfolk County, Virginia. Barnes' military service records show that he was twenty-three years old at the time of his enlistment. He gave his occupation as a farmer.

In June 1864, the Army of the Potomac under Lieutenant General Ulysses Grant had laid siege to General Robert E. Lee's Army of Northern Virginia in the lines around Petersburg. It was now September and the siege seemed to be no closer to accomplishing its purpose than when it had first started. General Grant ordered Major General Benjamin F. Butler, the commander of the Army of the James, to attack the Richmond defenses from the southeast. The attack would include infantry and cavalry, and would have two objectives: first, to force Lee to weaken his Petersburg defenses by drawing troops from there to repel Butler's attack, and second, to capture Richmond if possible.

General Butler was a strong advocate of enlisting black troops and his attacking columns included 14 regiments of black soldiers, primarily the United States Colored Troops. General Butler felt that other than General Smith's use of Hink's colored division in the assaults of June 15, the Colored troops had not yet been given a chance to show their valor or staying qualities. His U.S.C.T. were reasonably well trained and were well rested. "I want to convince myself," he told General Grant in discussing his plan, "whether, under my own eye, the Negro troops will fight; and if I can take, with the Negroes, a redoubt that turned Hancock's corps on a former occasion, that will settle the question."

To further demonstrate his point that black troops could fight just as well as white soldiers, General Butler assigned General Charles Paine's black division from the XVII Corps to attack the center of the Confederate line.

Private Barnes is one of the thirteen African American soldiers who earned the Medal of Honor at the battle of New Market Heights (Chapin's Farm) on September 29, 1864. The attack on the Rebel works at New Market Heights was one of the most stubborn of the war, with the bulk of the fighting being done by black troops, who sustained more than 50 percent casualties in a determined attack upon the enemy fortifications. The black troops had been asked to take a strong position protected in the front by two lines of abatis and one line of palisades, and in the rear of which was a lot of men who knew how to shoot. The Texans of Gregg's Brigade poured out a deadly hailstorm of bullets, which swept the leaves from the trees and cut down the black soldiers by the score.

Private Barnes pressed forward against this storm of lead, through all the obstacles and, although wounded, was one of the first to enter the enemy works. For this act of valor Private Barnes was awarded the Medal of Honor.

Barnes service records at the National Archives in Washington, D.C., show the following: Private Barnes was wounded at the Battle of New Market Heights on September 29, 1864. Barnes was promoted to Sergeant on July 1, 1865.

Sergeant Barnes remained in the army after the end of the Civil War. On December 24, 1866, William H. Barnes died of consumption at Indianola, Texas, at the Army Hospital. He is buried in the San Antonio National Cemetery at San Antonio, Texas.

1st Sergeant Powhatan Beaty, USA

5th U.S. Colored Troops

Powhatan Beaty was born on October 8, 1837, at Richmond, Richmond County, Virginia. In 1849, Beaty moved to Cincinnati. He had previously served in 1862 with the Cincinnati "Black Brigade." On June 7, 1863, Beaty enlisted as a private in Company G, 5th U.S. Colored Troops at Cincinnati, Hamilton County, Ohio. Born a slave, on his enlistment papers Beaty indicated that he had become "Free on or before April 19, 1861." Beaty gave his age as 24 years and his occupation as a turner. Beaty earned a promotion to sergeant on June 9, 1863.

Sergeant Beaty is one of the thirteen African American soldiers who earned the Medal of Honor at the battle of New Market Heights (Chapin's Farm) on September 29, 1864. The attack on the Rebel works at New Market Heights was one of the most stubborn of the war, with the bulk of the fighting being done by black troops, who sustained more than 50 percent casualties in the determined charge. The black troops had been asked to take a strong position, protected in the front by two lines of abatis and one line of palisades, and in the rear of which were a lot of men who knew how to shoot. The Texans of Gregg's Brigade poured out a deadly hailstorm of bullets which swept the leaves from the trees, and cut down the black soldiers by the score.

As the initial attack stalled at the abatis in front of the Confederate works, Colonel Draper tried to get the men to continue the charge, but his orders could not be heard over the roar of the battle.

As Company G retreated after the initial advance, the unit's color bearer was killed. Sergeant Beaty returned about 600 yards through enemy fire to pick up the flag and bring it back to the Company.

All along the lines, white officers were being shot down. Lieutenant Colonel Shirtliff, commander of the 5th U.S.C.T., was mortally wounded. At this critical point in the battle black soldiers rose from the ranks to replace the white officers who had been killed or wounded. Former slave Sergeant Powhatan Beaty took command of what was left of Company G, and gallantly led it forward against the Confederate works, despite severe casualties.

As a direct result of the courage of men like Sergeant Beaty, the black soldiers surged forward and took the Rebel works. When they met the enemy face to face, black men with arms of iron fought Southern white solders hand to hand with desperate valor. In the end, it was those who held the philosophy that black men were inferior and fit only to be the slaves of other men who were driven from the field.

Powhatan Beaty survived the war and returned to Cincinnati where he raised his family. His son, A. Lee Beaty, was a two-time Ohio Legislator and the first black assistant U.S. Attorney General for the Southern District of Ohio.

Powhatan Beaty died December 16, 1916. He is buried in the Union Baptist Cemetery at Cincinnati, Ohio.

Contraband Robert Blake, USN

U.S.S. Marblehead

Robert Blake was the first black man to earn the Navy's Medal of Honor. He was born a slave in South Santee, South Carolina. Blake was freed when the Blake plantation was burned during a Union Naval expedition up the Santee River in June 1862. About 400 slaves from the Blake Plantation were taken aboard the Union vessels and transported to North Island, in Winyah Bay. While Robert Blake was at North Island, Commander Prentiss requested 20 single men to serve aboard the U.S.S. *Vermont.* Robert Blake was among those who "volunteered" and was given the status "contraband."

Robert Blake earned the Medal of Honor on December 25, 1863, off Legareville, Stono River, John's Island, South Carolina. Robert Blake was serving as a steward for Lieutenant Commander Richard W. Mead, Jr. At about 5:00 A.M. , a howitzer shell, fired by the Rebels on John's Island, rocked the ship. Lieutenant Commander Mead jumped out of his bunk and rushed to his battle station on the quarter-deck still wearing his night clothes. Blake followed his commander, carrying his uniform, and insisting that he get dressed. Struggling to pull on his uniform Commander Mead shouted the order, "Man the guns. Commence firing." More shells rocked the ship as the Confederate gunners found their range and poured a heavy volume of fire onto the ship.

Blake, after delivering the uniform, went to the gun deck. Just as he arrived on the gun deck, a shell exploded sending him flying. Blake, bruised, got back on his feet, but the same shell that had sent Blake sprawling had killed the powder boy who had been serving one of the guns. Blake had no assigned duties during combat and could have returned to the relative safety of his quarters. Instead, he decided to take the place of the dead powder boy. Blake stripped to the waist, grabbed gunpowder boxes, and ran with them to the gun loaders. In the midst of the death and chaos of his first action, Blake performed with such calm determination that he impressed and inspired all those around him.

When Commander Mead saw Blake running back and forth with the gunpowder boxes, he asked what Blake was doing. Blake stopped for a second to reply, "Went down to the rocks to hide my face, but the rocks said there is no hiding place here. So here I am Sir." With that, Blake went back to his self-assigned duties.

On April 16, 1864, Blake was awarded the Medal of Honor. His citation reads as follows:

> On board the U.S. Steam Gunboat *Marblehead* off Legare-ville, Stono River, December 25, 1863, in an engagement with the enemy on John's Island. Serving the rifle gun, Blake, an escaped slave, carried out his duties bravely throughout the engagement, which resulted in the enemy's abandonment of positions, leaving a caisson and one gun behind.

Blake was promoted to seaman after the battle at John's Island. He completed the term of his enlistment and then re-enlisted, serving again aboard the *Vermont*.

1st Sergeant James H. Bronson, USA

5th U.S. Colored Troops

James H. Bronson was born in 1838 at Indiana County, Pennsylvania. He enlisted on August 3, 1863, as a private in Company D, 5th U.S. Colored Troops, at Trumbell County, Ohio.

Sergeant Bronson is one of the thirteen African American soldiers who earned the Medal of Honor at the battle of New Market Heights (Chapin's Farm) on September 29, 1864. The attack on the Rebel works at New Market Heights was one of the most stubborn of the war. The Confederate force of 1,800 men was badly outnumbered by the attacking Federal force, which totaled 13,000 men. But the Confederates held the high ground and, in addition to making rifle pits, the Confederates covered their position with two lines of abatis to delay and entangle the attacking soldiers. One line of abatis was constructed of felled trees with branches facing the enemy, tops lopped off to snag the Union soldiers' clothing and expose them to gunfire. Closer to the entrenchments was a second line of abatis parallel to the first. Much of it was a *Chevaux-de-frise*, a dangerous-looking impediment made by boring holes in logs and embedding rows of sharpened timbers. Behind the two lines of abatis was a line of palisades, and in the rear these fortifications were Robert E. Lee's "grenadier guards" — the 1st, 4th and 5th Texas and the 3rd Arkansas regiments of infantry. Brigadier General John Gregg commanded this Brigade.

As the initial attack stalled at the abatis in front of the Confederate works, the Texans of Gregg's Brigade poured out a deadly hailstorm of bullets, which swept the leaves from the trees, and cut down the black soldiers by the score. Colonel Draper tried to get the men to continue the charge, but his orders could not be heard over the roar of the battle. The Confederates, believing that the colored soldiers would not stand under fire on their own, concentrated their fire on the white officers. Lieutenant Colonel Shirtliff, commander of the 5th U.S.C.T., was mortally wounded. All of the white officers in Company D were also killed or wounded. But the black soldiers did not run.

As the last of the white officers in Company D were shot down, former slave Sergeant James H. Bronson took command of the company and rallied his men. Then Sergeant Bronson, placing himself in the front of the line, led his men forward against the Confederate works.

The black soldiers, angry at the losses they had endured, surged over the abatis and the palisades. They took the rifle pits in hand-to-hand combat. The strength of the Confederate position and the intensity of the battle were demonstrated by the disproportionately high Union casualties. The Confederates lost some 50 casualties in the battle compared to 850 suffered by the Union forces.

Bronson's relations with the Army appear to have been stormy after he received his Medal of Honor. His military service records at the National Archives in Washington, D.C., show that, from June 20, 1865, Bronson was in confinement at Fort Totten, North Carolina, and that on September 19, 1865, Bronson was in the custody of the Provost Marshall of the Middle Military Department as a deserter. Bronson was mustered out of the service on September 20, 1865, at Carolina City, North Carolina.

James H. Bronson died March 16, 1884. Bronson is buried in the Chartiers Cemetery at Carnegie, Pennsylvania.

Landsman William H. Brown, USN

U.S.S. Brooklyn

Grave of Landsman William H. Brown, USN

William H. Brown was born in 1836 at Baltimore, Baltimore County, Maryland. On March 26, 1864, a 28-year-old William H. Brown enlisted in the Navy from Maryland. Brown was given the rank of Landsman, which is the rank given to inexperienced men when they first join the Navy. Landsman Brown was assigned to serve aboard the U.S.S. *Brooklyn*, which was part of the Gulf blockade fleet under the command of Rear Admiral David Farragut.

Landsman William H. Brown

was one of the four African Americans who earned the Medal of Honor on August 5, 1864, at the Battle of Mobile Bay, Alabama. Further details concerning the action at Mobile Bay are given in the record of Landsman John Lawson. William H. Brown's citation reads as follows:

> On board the U.S.S. *Brooklyn* during successful attacks against Fort Morgan, rebel gunboats and the ram *Tennessee* in Mobile Bay on August 5, 1864. Stationed in the immediate vicinity of the shell whips, which were twice cleared of men by bursting shells, Brown remained steadfast at his post and performed his duties in the powder division throughout the furious action, which resulted in the surrender of the prize rebel ram *Tennessee* and in the damaging and destruction of the batteries of Fort Morgan.

William H. Brown died November 5, 1896. He is buried in Arlington National Cemetery, Arlington, Virginia, where a special headstone marks his grave.

Landsman Wilson Brown, USN

U.S.S. Hartford

Wilson Brown was born in 1841 at Natchez, Adams County, Mississippi. Brown enlisted in the Navy along the Mississippi River, in Mississippi. He served aboard the U.S.S. *Hartford.*

On the morning of August 5, 1864, the *Hartford* led a fleet of 14 Union ships past the blazing guns of forts Gaines, Morgan and Powell into Mobile Bay. No sooner had the *Hartford* run the gauntlet of the forts than the Confederate ram *Tennessee* attacked. The *Hartford* responded with her nine-inch smooth-bore guns and a full fledged navel battle was in progress.

Below the gun deck, Landsman John Lawson, Landsman Wilson Brown and four other sailors, sweat pouring down their bodies, were tugging with all their might on the shell whip. Suddenly, an enemy shell exploded in the midst of the six man crew. Four of the crewmen were killed instantly. Lawson was violently thrown against the bulkhead of the ship. Landsman Brown was knocked off the birth deck and was thrown through the hatchway to the lower deck where he was knocked unconscious. As

Lawson lay slumped against the bulkhead stunned by the blast. As he began to gather his wits about him, he noticed his left leg felt numb. Lawson tried to stand but was unable to get up. He could not see his leg and for a moment he thought it had been shot off. As his head continued to clear, he was relieved to find that he was sitting on his leg. A medic came onto the scene and found Landsman Lawson the only man alive on the deck. Lawson's leg was bleeding from a deep shrapnel wound. When he tried to take Lawson below for treatment Lawson refused saying, "The guns must be served first!" With that remark Lawson returned to his duties at the shell whip. Ignoring the pain and the shells bursting around him, Lawson concentrated on doing his duty.

Wilson Brown regained consciousness, crawling out from under the body of a dead man who had fallen on top of him. He promptly returned to the shell whip on the berth deck. For the remainder of the battle, which lasted several hours, Lawson and Wilson pulled the whip. This was the only means of supplying the gun crew above.

Both Lawson and Brown were awarded the Medal of Honor for their valor aboard the *Hartford* during the battle of Mobile Bay, two of the six African Americans who earned the Navy Medal of Honor during the Civil War.

Landsman Wilson Brown's citation reads as follows:

> On board the flagship U.S.S. *Hartford*, during successful attacks against Fort Morgan, rebel gunboats and the ram *Tennessee* in Mobile Bay, August 5, 1864. Knocked unconscious into the hold of the ship when an enemy shell burst fatally wounded the man on the ladder above him, Brown upon regaining consciousness promptly returned to the shell whip on the berth deck and zealously continued to perform his duties, although four of the six men at his station had been killed or wounded by the enemy's terrific fire.

Wilson Brown died January 24, 1900. He is buried in National Cemetery, Natchez, Mississippi.

Sergeant William Harvey Carney, USA

54th Massachusetts Infantry

As the 650 officers and men of the 54th Massachusetts stood in line ready to commence the assault on Fort Wagner, they knew that the issue was in doubt. It was not just the issue of whether or not Fort Wagner could be taken or whether or not the Union would win the war. The answers to those questions would not be proven on this day. The issue to be tested this very evening was whether or not black troops could be trusted to fight alongside their white brothers.

The men of the 54th Massachusetts were the first regiment in line and were assigned to lead the assault on Fort Wagner. Colonel Robert Gould Shaw, the 25-year-old Colonel of the 54th, had volunteered his men for this "post of honor," hoping to prove the mettle of the U.S. Army's showcase black regiment. "The eyes of thousands will look on what you do tonight," Colonel Shaw had told his men just before he drew his sword and led them forward into battle.

Sergeant William H. Carney, USA

For more than seven hours, Fort Wagner had undergone a terrific bombardment from the Union Navy offshore and all of the artillery that General Quincy Gilmore could muster on the land. The storm of shot and shell had been so heavy that one witness said that enough ammunition had been expended to establish several first class iron foundries. In truth, the bombardment had had very little effect. Only thirteen of the 1700 man garrison had been killed or wounded during the barrage and none of the fort's guns had been put out of action. Those guns were still standing double-shotted with canister and sited to sweep all of the approaches to the fort.

When the barrage stopped, Colonel Shaw gave the order to advance. Before the signal was given to double their pace, the men of the 54th were hit with a torrent of shot and shell from the combined batteries of Fort Wagner, Fort Sumter and Battery Gregg. The black soldiers were mowed down like grass, but Colonel Shaw and the survivors of the 54th did not waiver. Closing ranks on the colors, they pressed the attack forward. The soldiers of the 54th gained Fort Wagner's parapet and held it for an hour in the flame-stabbed darkness before they were forced to fall back.

Union casualties were heavy. Of the 650 men engaged, the 54th Massachusetts lost 272, including Colonel Shaw, who was shot through the heart just as he mounted Wagner's parapet. No one who witnessed the charge would ever question the courage of the 54th or any of the regiments that charged across that fire-swept stretch of sand. Sergeant William H. Carney earned the Medal of Honor for his actions during the charge.

William H. Carney was born a slave, the son of William Carney and Ann (Dean) Carney, in Norfolk, Norfolk County, Virginia, on February 29, 1840. Ann Carney was a slave owned by a Major Carney. William Carney, Sr., was a free man. When his master died, William H. Carney, age fourteen, was manumitted.

It was illegal to educate blacks in the South prior to the Civil War, but some men of conscience set up secret schools to teach blacks how to read and write. At the age of fourteen, Carney began to attend one such secret school run by a minister. When he was fifteen years old, he became a Christian and his life's ambition was to become a Christian minister. Freed by his master's last will and testament upon Major Carney's death, William Carney, Sr., moved his family north. Both William Carney, Sr., and his son spent time as seamen before settling down in New Bedford, Massachusetts.

Carney supported himself in New Bedford doing odd jobs, but Carney's first choice was always to become a Christian minister. Carney joined a church in New Bedford and studied for the ministry. Then in late 1862, the call came from Governor Andrew for a regiment of black Union troops. Carney decided to postpone his plans for the ministry and immediately volunteered. He later explained that he felt being a soldier and serving God were compatible: "I felt I could best serve my God by serving my country and my oppressed brothers."

On February 17, 1863, a 23-year-old Carney enlisted in Company C, 54th Massachusetts Infantry. Five months after his enlistment, Sergeant Carney earned the Medal of Honor at Fort Wagner, South Carolina, becoming the first of eighteen African American soldiers to earn the Medal of Honor during the Civil War.

On July 18, 1863, the Union forces were drawn up outside of Fort

Wagner in South Carolina. The taking of Fort Wagner was considered essential to the capture of Charleston. At noon, the Union artillery opened fire upon the fort. The bombardment was joined by six iron-clads, firing on the fort from the bay. The 54th Massachusetts was the first regiment line, with the 6th Connecticut immediately behind them. The 54th advanced to within one thousand yards of the fort through a hailstorm of lead and steel, and then took cover in the sand waiting for the order to advance. At 7:45 P.M., Colonel Shaw calmly walked along the front to the center of the line and gave the order "Attention." The men of the 54th sprang to their feet, and at double time charged into a fire-storm of musket and cannon fire.

As soon as the 54th began its advance, men began to fall under the musketry, shell and canister being fired at them. Sergeant John Wall, the color bearer, was wounded by a shell burst. Sergeant Carney seized the flag and moved to the front of the column. Carney advanced with the flag, the men of the 54th falling all around him, until he found himself alone at the fort's entrance. Carney did not dare enter the fort alone, so he hid on its outer slope. For half an hour, with shot and shell bursting all around him, musket balls and exploding grenades kicking up the sand, Carney hugged the slope of the fort.

Finally, the Union soldiers renewed the attack on the right and the Confederates' attention was directed away from him. As Carney moved away from the slope of the fort, he saw a group of soldiers coming towards him. Thinking they were Federal soldiers, Carney raised his flag and moved to join them. Suddenly he realized they were Rebels. Carney furled the flag and ran down the embankment into the ditch, which was filled with water up to his waist. Carney was still alone, all the men who had initially climbed the embankment with him being either dead or wounded.

As Carney fled towards the rear, he was shot twice. Sergeant Carney dashed on. On his way, Carney met a member of the 100th New York. The New Yorker asked Carney if he was wounded and upon receiving an affirmative response, treated his wounds and assisted him to the rear. Carney was struck again by a bullet, which grazed his head. As Carney struggled forward, the New Yorker offered to carry the flag. Carney refused stating that "No one but a member of the Fifty-fourth should carry the colors."

When Carney reached the Union lines, he was treated by medical corpsmen; Sergeant Carney had been shot in the breast, right arm and both legs, in addition to his head wound. Carney then went to the 54th's encampment. When his comrades saw him carrying the flag, they broke into a cheer. Sergeant Carney told the men, "Boys, I did my duty; the dear old flag never touched the ground!"

Sergeant Carney was discharged from the infantry with the rank of sergeant at Black Island, South Carolina, on June 30, 1864, for disability from the wounds he sustained.

After the war, Carney returned to New Bedford, where he was employed as a mail carrier until 1901. William Carney was a popular speaker at patriotic celebrations, including a convention of black veterans in 1887. Carney received the Medal of Honor on May 20, 1900. In 1901 Carney moved to Boston where he served as a messenger in the Massachusetts State House.

William H. Carney died on December 9, 1908, at New Bedford, Massachusetts. When he died, the flags at the Massachusetts State House were flown at half-mast — an honor which up to that time had been reserved solely for the passing away of governors and presidents. Carney is buried in the Oak Grove Cemetery, New Bedford, Massachusetts, where a special headstone indicates that he earned the Medal of Honor.

Seaman Clement Dees, USN

U.S.S. Pontoosuc

Clement Dees was born in about 1837 in San Antonio, Cape Verde Islands, off the West Coast of Africa. On June 6, 1864, Dees enlisted as Clement Dees, age 27, in the U.S. Navy for a two year enlistment aboard the U.S.S. *Pontoosuc*, which was docked at Eastport, Maine. Dees was described as a mulatto (colored) and his occupation was given as sailor. A total of 12 men enlisted on the *Pontoosuc*. Six of the men counted towards Eastport's draft quota. Clement Dees was one of these men.

Clement Dees earned the Medal of Honor during the period of December 4, 1864, to February 22, 1865, while serving aboard the U.S.S. *Pontoosuc* in operations in and around Cape Fear River, North Carolina, which included the bombardment and capture of Fort Fisher, North Carolina, and Wilmington, North Carolina.

On January 8, 1865, General Alfred Terry and 8000 men arrived at Beaufort, North Carolina. He immediately boarded the U.S.S. *Malvern* and, by direction of General Grant, laid his sealed orders before

Admiral Porter. "The siege of Fort Fisher," they read, " will not be abandoned until its reduction is accomplished."

Winter gales kept the vessels in port until the 12th when the combined armada steamed to Fort Fisher. The fighting fleet took its positions for bombardment. They deployed in three lines, with the ironclads on the angle of the Northeast bastion, giving enfilade fire along both axes of Fort Fisher, which was configured in the shape of a 7. To occupy the rebel gunners with smothering rapid fire, Admiral Porter added the U.S.S. *Brooklyn* to the ironclad division.

Commanding officers aboard all ships were cautioned to cut their fuses and shoot carefully. There had been an element of wildness in the first action against Fort Fisher which Admiral Porter did not want repeated. "The object," Porter noted, "is to lodge the shell in the parapets and tear away the traverses" over the bombproof shelters. No vessel was to retire from her place in the line "unless in a sinking condition." When the troops were ready to assault, he would hoist signal "2211" and blast a steam whistle which was to be repeated by every ship in the fleet.

At first light, January 13, the fleet opened a deliberate, concentrated, all day barrage. At 8:30 A.M. the first wave of Terry's troops pulled for the beach well north of the land face of the fort. The first landing was made with over two hundred boats. As soon as the order was given to land, the boats went for the beach at full speed. Rebel shells were splashing among the boats and the bullets were spluttering on the surface of the water, but the boats never faltered.

The soldiers had some difficulty in getting out with dry feet, and many of them rolled in the surf. But once on shore, it was glorious to see how they knew their business. As soon as they got to their feet, they spread out into a skirmish line, and the rifles began to crack. By mid afternoon, General Terry's entire force was ashore with entrenching gear and 20 days supplies.

Through the night and all the next day (the 14th) the fleet kept up its intense bombardment of the fort. At 11:30 A.M. on the 15th, the bombardment concentrated on the short land face of the fort, and was so effective that it dismounted all but one of the Rebel's guns. The parapets and traverses were torn apart and the wooden stockade was breached or knocked down in several places. The wires to the minefields surrounding the fort were totally obliterated. Never before had a fleet accomplished so much destruction of a fortified position, nor would any fleet match the devastation again until the great amphibious invasions of World War II.

By gradual approaches, the army worked down the far river side of Confederate Point, against the open, short axis of Fort Fisher. At each forward movement, the leading brigade entrenched, while the rear brigades occupied the former positions. By this leapfrogging, the army advanced to within range of the position for their final rush.

Not willing to allow the army to have the lion-sized share of the credit for the capture of Fort Fisher, Admiral Porter had mustered a naval brigade of 1,600 sailors and 400 marines, under the command of Chief of Staff K. R. Breese. The sailors were armed with cutlasses and revolvers. Admiral Porter was certain that 2000 good men from the fleet would carry the fort.

The naval brigade landed at 1:00 P.M. on the 15th in the wrong place — a mile and a half away from the bastion they were intended to attack. The sailors moved forward in three divisions with the marines leading the way. At 3:00 P.M., the steam whistles of the fleet sounded, signaling the general advance on the fort. The sailors charged across the last 1,200 yards, all of it loose sand, under an intense fire from the fort. The Confederates considered the assault of the naval brigade to be the main assault and concentrated the fire of the entire garrison upon the oncoming sailors. The sailors' line broke under the intense fire and the assault failed. More than 300 sailors and marines were killed in the attack.

The Confederate commander, Colonel Lamb, was congratulating himself on his success in repulsing the assault, when three U.S. flags suddenly appeared over the other bastion wall and blueclad soldiers came pouring through the gap. The attack of the naval brigade had served to divert the attention of the Rebels until it was too late.

The battle degenerated into hand-to-hand combat as the Federals drove the Rebels from traverse to traverse and from trench to trench. At 9:00 P.M., the defense of the fort collapsed and the Confederates surrendered. Nineteen hundred Rebel prisoners and forty-four heavy guns fell to the Union.

Seaman Clement Dees was one of the sailors who participated in the attack on Fort Fisher. His commanding officer, Commander William G. Temple, recommended to Rear Admiral Porter that Dees be awarded the Medal of Honor for, "gallantry, skill, and coolness in action...."

Department General Order No. 59, dated June 22, 1865, stated, "Awarded Medal of Honor to: Clement Dees, Seaman (colored), *Pontoosuc*." Clement Dees' name does not appear, however, upon the rolls of those who have received the Medal of Honor. Seaman Dees never received his medal. After the medal was approved but before it was awarded, Clement Dees deserted from the Navy. He deserted on July 22, 1865, from the U.S.S. *Ohio,* a receiving ship then anchored in Boston Harbor. The Civil War had ended in April 1865. By July 1865, Dees was sitting in a receiving ship waiting to be discharged. For some reason or another, Dees did not wait to be formally discharged but chose to desert.

Both Dees' decision and action were not uncommon. In the summer of 1865 many soldiers and sailors were tired of waiting for their official discharge and they just went home. Nevertheless, as a result of the "desertion" the Navy forfeited Dees' Medal of Honor.

Five other persons also forfeited an award of Medals of Honor through desertion. Clement Dees and these other deserters may never have realized that, in 1865, they had been awarded the nation's highest military medal for heroism.

Sergeant Decatur Dorsey, USA

39th U.S. Colored Troops

Decatur Dorsey was born a slave in 1836 at Howard County, Maryland. On March 22, 1864, a 25-year-old Dorsey enlisted in the Army at Baltimore, Maryland, as a private in Company B, 39th U.S. Colored Troops. He stated that his occupation at the time of enlistment was that of a laborer.

Dorsey's military service records at the National Archives in Washington, D.C., show that Dorsey was promoted to Corporal on May 17, 1864.

Sergeant Dorsey earned the Medal of Honor on July 30, 1864, at Petersburg, Virginia, during the Battle of the Crater. Grant's Army of the Potomac had chased General Lee to Petersburg, where the Army of Northern Virginia had taken up defensive positions in the strong works surrounding the city.

One attempt to breach the works and take the city occurred on July 30, 1864. A tunnel over 500 feet long had been dug under the Rebel works. At 4:45 A.M., over four tons of gunpowder exploded, blowing a huge crater into the Confederate lines. A Union division rushed into the gap, but the attack faltered as the men stayed in the crater. Two other divisions advanced but they also failed to advance out of the crater. The failure to move out of the crater proved fatal to the attack and many of the attackers. The Confederates reorganized and returned to the lip of the crater where they shot down into the massed Union soldiers like shooting fish in a barrel.

About 7:30 A.M., the reserve division of black troops was sent into the battle, after the assault by the white troops had stalled. The Colored Troops marched into total chaos. From their front came a heavy volume of musket fire, and on both flanks the Rebels were pouring in canister and grape shot from their artillery. The black troops had to open their ranks to allow fleeing white troops to get through; immediately thereafter, the black troops charged. Sergeant Dorsey, the color-sergeant of the 39th U.S.C.T., advanced in front of his charging regiment and planted his colors on the Rebel works. When his regiment was forced to retreat, Sergeant Dorsey retrieved his flag, and rallied the men around the colors for a second charge.

The black troops rallied around their colors and, with a deep throated "Hurrah," surged forward again. This time, the momentum of the charge took them up over the Confederate works, where they engaged the Rebels in hand-to-hand combat. The black troops captured 200 prisoners and two stands of colors before they were forced to retreat in the face of a determined Confederate counterattack.

After the second assault was driven back, General Ambrose Burnside ordered a withdrawal. He later explained in his report that the men had become disorganized, being largely without leaders. The black troops had fought valiantly. This fact was demonstrated by their casualties which totaled 1324 men, more than any other division participating in the battle.

Dorsey was promoted to sergeant on August 1, 1864, and was promoted to 1st sergeant on January 1, 1865. Sergeant Dorsey was mustered out of the service on December 4, 1865, at Wilmington, North Carolina.

After the war, Decatur Dorsey moved to Hoboken, New Jersey, where he lived with his wife. Dorsey died July 11, 1891, at Hoboken. He is buried in the Flower Hill Cemetery in North Bergen, New Jersey.

Sergeant Christian A. Fleetwood, USA

4th U.S. Colored Troops

Christian Abraham Fleetwood was born to free African American parents on July 21, 1840, at Baltimore, Baltimore County, Maryland. Fleetwood

Christian Fleetwood, USA

graduated from the Ashmun Institute, which later became Lincoln University, in Pennsylvania. He enlisted on August 11, 1863, at Baltimore as a private in Company G, 4th U.S. Colored Troops. The patriotic Fleetwood later explained that he had enlisted "to save the country from ruin." Fleetwood was promoted to sergeant on August 19, 1863, and served continuously in that rank until mustered out of the service on May 9, 1866.

Sergeant Fleetwood served with his regiment at Yorktown, Pennsylvania, and Fort Fisher, North Carolina. At the end of December 1864, Fleetwood recorded his thoughts concerning being a soldier in his diary:

This year has brought about many changes that at the beginning were or would have been thought impossible. The close of the year finds me a soldier for the cause of my race. May God bless the cause, and enable me in the coming year to forward it on.

Sergeant Fleetwood is one of the thirteen African American soldiers who earned the Medal of Honor on September 29, 1864, at the battle of New Market Heights. The battle was opened early in the morning by the 4th and 6th U.S. Colored troops under the command of Brigadier General S. A. Duncan. All along the lines the white officers were singled out and shot down by the Confederates defending the heights. When all the white officers had been killed or wounded, the black non-commissioned officers stepped forward to take command of companies. Sergeant Fleetwood took command of the entire left half of the line of the 4th

U.S.C.T. He led his new command forward in a charge against the Rebel positions only to see the regiment cut to pieces. Fleetwood recorded that men fell "as hailstones sweep the leaves from the trees."

When the charge upon the Rebel works commenced, the 4th U.S.C.T. had eleven officers and 350 men. A color guard of two sergeants and ten corporals protected the colors. One of the color sergeants was shot down, the bullet breaking the staff and passing through his body. Sergeant Alfred B. Hilton took the flag and pressed forward carrying both stands of colors. During the advance, Sergeant Hilton was shot through the leg. As he fell, Hilton held up the colors and shouted: "Boys save the colors!" Eleven of the twelve members of the color guard were shot down, and anyone touching the flag became a primary target for the Rebels. Before the flags touched the ground, Corporal Veal took the regimental colors from Sergeant Hilton and Sergeant Fleetwood took the national colors. Together they rallied their men around the flags.

Concerning the engagement Fleetwood said:

> I have never been able to understand how Veal and I lived under such a hail of bullets, unless it was because we were both such little fellows. I think I weighed then about 125 pounds and Veal about the same. We did not get a scratch. A bullet passed between my legs, cutting my boot-leg trousers and even my stockings without breaking the skin.

Men in battle recognize courage when they see it. Following the Battle of New Market Heights, a petition, signed by every officer in his regiment, was sent to Secretary of War Edwin Stanton, calling for Fleetwood to become a commissioned officer. Bureaucrats who sit behind desks, however, follow rules, regulations and conform to policies. Due to the policy against making African Americans officers, the petition was ignored by the War Department.

Christian Fleetwood, in a letter to Dr. James Hall, explained his decision to leave the Army once the war was over. Fleetwood explained that he had joined the army and faced the dangers of war to help his race. He had been led to believe or hope that black soldiers, upon evidence of merit and ability, would be promoted to the rank of company and regimental officers. When these representations proved false, he was no long willing to stay in the Army.

> I see no good that will result to our people by continuing to serve, on the contrary it seems to me that our continuing

to act in a subordinate capacity, with no hope of advancement
or promotion is an absolute injury to our cause. It is a tacit
but telling acknowledgment on our part that we are not fit
for promotion, & that we are satisfied to remain in a state of
marked and acknowledged subserviency.

After the war, Fleetwood was active in the District of Columbia
National Guard, in which he rose to the rank of major before his retirement.
Christian A. Fleetwood died September 28, 1914, at Washington,
D.C. He is buried at Harmony Memorial Park, Landover, Maryland.

Private James Gardiner, USA

36th U.S. Colored Troops

James Daniel Gardner was born on September 16, 1839, at Gloucester, Gloucester County, Virginia. On September 15, 1863, he enlisted
under the name of James "Gardiner," in Company I, 36th U.S. Colored
Troops, at Yorktown, York County, Virginia. At the time of his enlistment, Gardiner stated that his occupation was that of an oysterman.

Private Gardiner is one of the thirteen African Americans who
earned the Medal of Honor on September 29, 1864, at the battle of
New Market Heights (Chapin's Farm). The attack on the Rebel works at
New Market Heights was one of the most stubborn of the war, with the
bulk of the fighting being done by black troops, who sustained more
than 50 percent casualties in the determined charge. The black troops
had been asked to take a strong position protected in the front by two
lines of abatis and one line of palisades, and in the rear of which were a
lot of experienced shooters. The Texans of Gregg's Brigade poured out
a deadly hailstorm of bullets and cut down the black soldiers by the
score.

As the initial attack stalled at the abatis in front of the Confederate works, Colonel Draper tried to get the men to continue the charge,
but his orders could not be heard over the roar of the battle. Lines of
black soldiers stood their ground and exchanged volley for volley with
Confederates who were well protected behind a palisade. This was a losing proposition for the black soldiers, who needed to continue the charge
against the Rebel positions in order to have any chance of winning the
battle.

All along the lines, the white officers leading the black troops were being particularly singled out by the Confederate marksmen and many were being killed and wounded. This was particularly true in the 5th U.S.C.T. Lieutenant Colonel Shirtliff, commander of the 5th U.S.C.T., was mortally wounded. At this critical point in the battle, black soldiers stepped forward from the ranks and took command of companies, replacing the white officers who had been killed or wounded.

When all of the white officers in Company C, 5th U.S.C.T. had been shot down, Sergeant Milton Holland, a 20-year-old former slave from Austin, Texas, took command of that company. Sergeant Powhatan Beaty, a former slave, also stepped forward and took command of Company G, 5th U.S.C.T., while Sergeant James Bronson, a Virginia born 19-year-old from Pennsylvania, led Company D, 5th U.S.C.T., and Sergeant Robert Pinn, an Ohio farmer, took command of Company I, 5th U.S.C.T.

Inspired by the courage and example of such men as Holland, Beaty, Bronson and Pimm, the black soldiers surged forward and overwhelmed the Rebel defenses. Leading the charge and the first to enter the works were Sergeant James H. Harris, Sergeant Edward Ratcliff and Private William H. Barnes of the 38th U.S.C.T. and Private James Gardiner of the 36th U.S.C.T.

Private Gardiner demonstrated his courage by rushing in advance of his brigade. As the Rebel line began to break under the pressure of the Union attack, Private Gardiner shot a Rebel officer, who was on the parapet rallying his men. Charging into the works, Private Gardiner ran the same officer through with a bayonet. The black soldiers followed Gardiner into the Rebel works where they met the enemy face to face. In advancing against the fortified Confederate positions under intense fire and in the hand-to-hand combat that followed, Private Gardiner and the black warriors who followed him into the Confederate works both demonstrated their valor and cast their votes for equality of the black race.

The day after the battle, Private Gardiner was promoted to sergeant. His military service records at the National Archives in Washington, D.C., show that he was subsequently reduced in rank from sergeant to private on July 13, 1865. He must have committed some other infraction of military rules since he was placed in confinement at Brazos Santiago, Texas, on March 29, 1866. Private Gardiner was mustered out of the service at Brazos Santiago, Texas, on September 20, 1866, having served his country and his race faithfully and well.

James Daniel "Gardner" died on September 29, 1905, at Clark's Summit, Pennsylvania. He is buried at Calvary Crest Cemetery, Ottumwa, Iowa.

Sergeant James H. Harris, USA

38th U.S. Colored Troops

James H. Harris was born in 1828, at St Mary's County, Maryland. He was a 36-year-old farmer when he enlisted as a private in Company B, 38th U.S. Colored Troops at Great Mills, St Mary's County, Maryland, on February 14, 1864. Private Harris was promoted to corporal on July 25, 1864, and Corporal Harris was promoted to sergeant September 10, 1864, just 19 days before the Battle of New Market Heights.

Sergeant Harris was one of the thirteen African Americans who earned the Medal of Honor at the battle of New Market Heights (Chapin's Farm) on September 29, 1864. The attack on the Rebel works at New Market Heights was one of the most stubborn of the war, with the bulk of the fighting being done by black troops, who sustained more than 50 percent casualties in the determined charge. The black troops had been asked to take a strong position protected in the front by two lines of abatis and one line of palisades, and in the rear of which were a lot of men who knew how to shoot. The Texans of Gregg's Brigade poured out a deadly hailstorm of bullets and cut down the black soldiers by the score.

As the initial attack stalled at the abatis in front of the Confederate works, Colonel Draper tried to get the men to continue the charge, but his orders could not be heard over the

Grave of Sergeant James H. Harris, USA

roar of the battle. All along the lines, white officers were being shot down. Lieutenant Colonel Shirtliff, commander of the 5th U.S.C.T., was mortally wounded. At this critical point in the battle, black soldiers rose from the ranks to replace the white officers who had been killed or wounded.

Sergeant Milton Holland, a 20-year-old former slave from Austin, Texas, took command of Company C. Richmond born Sergeant Powhatan Beaty, a former slave, took command of Company G. Sergeant James Bronson, a Virginia born 19-year-old from Pennsylvania, led Company D. Sergeant Robert Pinn, a 21-year-old Ohio farmer, who was the son of a run away slave, took command of Company I.

Leadership having been restored, it was vital that the stalled attack get moving again. It was suicide for the black soldiers to attempt to shoot it out with the Rebels so long as the Rebels were in well-protected positions and the black soldiers were out in the open. When the black non-commissioned officers ordered the men forward, Sergeant James H. Harris, Sergeant Edward Radcliff and Private William H. Barnes took the lead in charging the enemy works. Out in front of the lines, which were again moving forward, they became the focus of the enemy fire, but they did not waiver.

These three men were the first to enter the Rebel works and engage the Confederates in hand-to-hand combat. They were followed close behind by the remainders of companies and regiments. Soon the pressure on the Confederate positions became overwhelming and the surviving Rebels fled the field.

Sergeant Harris' military service records show that he was wounded on September 29, 1864, at the Battle of New Market Heights. Harris was reduced in rank to private on July 1, 1865, and was mustered out of the service on January 25, 1867, at Indianola, Texas.

James H. Harris died on January 28, 1898. He is buried in the Arlington National Cemetery at Arlington, Virginia, where a special headstone identifies his grave as the final resting place of a Medal of Honor recipient.

Private Thomas R. Hawkins, USA

6th U.S. Colored Troops

Thomas R. Hawkins was born in 1840 in Cincinnati, Hamilton County, Ohio. On August 4, 1863, Hawkins enlisted in the 6th

U.S. Colored Troops, an African American regiment raised in Pennsylvania.

Private Hawkins earned the Medal of Honor on July 21, 1864, at the battle of Deep Bottom. Private Hawkins' simple citation reads as follows: "Rescue of regimental colors." No further information concerning Private Hawkins' exploit is known.

At the battle of Deep Bottom, Virginia, four black regiments fought with intrepidity in one of the fiercest campaigns of the battle for Virginia. The black soldiers defiantly withstood the Rebel assaults. Major General David B. Birney, the commander of the X Corps, said, concerning the stand of the African American troops, that "It was one of the most stirring and gallant affairs I have ever known."

Thomas R. Hawkins died on February 28, 1870, at Washington, D.C. He is buried at Harmony Cemetery, Landover, Maryland.

Sergeant Alfred B. Hilton, USA

4th U.S. Colored Troops

Alfred B. Hilton was born in 1842 at Harford County, Maryland. He enlisted at Baltimore, Maryland, as a private in Company H, 4th U.S. Colored Troops.

Sergeant Hilton is one of the thirteen African Americans who earned the Medal of Honor on September 29, 1864, at the battle of New Market Heights (Chapin's Farm), Virginia. When the 4th U.S.C.T. advanced against the Confederate works that morning, Sergeant Hilton was one of the color sergeants carrying the national colors. The colored troops marched into a fire-storm of shot, shell and musket fire. Men fell on all sides, swept down by the intense Confederate fire.

When the color bearer carrying the regimental colors was shot down, Sergeant Hilton took up the colors, carrying both flags forward. Sergeant Hilton, a magnificent specimen of manhood — over 6 feet tall and splendidly proportioned — unflinchingly bore the banners forward. As the Confederate fire swept the field, Sergeant Hilton was shot through the leg. As he fell, he held up the flags and cried out, "Boys, save the colors!" Before they could touch the ground, the flags were taken by Corporal Veal and Sergeant Fleetwood and bravely born forward. Both men would also earn the Medal of Honor that day.

Hilton also received a medal for gallantry from Major General Benjamin Butler in addition to the Medal of Honor. The citation of the medal awarded by Butler reads as follows:

> Alfred H. Hilton, color Sergeant 4th U.S.C.T., the bearer of the national colors, when the color sergeant with the regimental standard fell beside him, seized the standard and struggled forward with both colors, until disabled with a severe wound at the enemy's inner line of abatis, and when on the ground he showed that his thoughts were for the colors and not for himself. He has a special medal for gallantry, and will have his warrant as first sergeant.

Sergeant Hilton did not get his promotion to first sergeant. Just twenty days after the battle, on October 21, 1864, Hilton died at Fortress Monroe, Virginia, of his wounds suffered at the battle of New Market Heights. He is buried in Hampton National Cemetery, Hampton, Virginia.

During the Civil War, only 33 of the 1,524 Medals of Honor awarded were awarded posthumously. The War Department had a dual purpose in awarding Medals of Honor. The medals were both for the purpose of recognizing bravery and for the purpose of boosting the morale of the men. The War Department felt that medals given to dead men did not serve to boost morale. The fact that a Medal of Honor was awarded posthumously to Sergeant Hilton for his valor at New Market Heights shows the magnitude of his act of valor.

Sergeant Milton M. Holland, USA

5th U.S. Colored Troops

Milton M. Holland was born a slave on August 1, 1844, at Austin, Travis County, Texas. In the late 1850s, Bird Holland, a longtime civil servant and former Secretary of State of the Republic of Texas, purchased Milton Holland and his two brothers and gave them their freedom. The three Holland brothers traveled north, putting distance between themselves and the Southern states and their damnable philosophy that one man could own another. The brothers ended up in Athens County, Ohio, where they attended Albany Enterprise Academy in Ohio.

It shows the complexity of the issues involved in the Civil War, that Bird Holland, a man who was willing to buy slaves just to give them their freedom, was later killed at the Battle of Sabine Cross Roads, wearing the uniform of a Confederate officer.

In 1861, when the war broke out, Milton Holland was attending school in Athens County, Ohio. Milton Holland immediately left school and attempted to enlist in the Army. He was rejected, however, because of his age. The war that was intended to free his race had started and Holland was determined to do his part. Rejected by the Army, Holland, sought employment with the quartermaster's office. He was accepted and served under Colonel Nelson H. Vorhis.

In June 1863, when blacks were finally allowed to serve in the Army, Holland enlisted as a private in Company C, 5th U.S. Colored Troops. The 5th U.S. Colored Troops was a regiment that was raised in Ohio and accredited to that state.

Sergeant Holland was one of the thirteen African Americans who earned the Medal of Honor at the Battle of New Market Heights (Chapin's Farm) on September 29, 1864. The attack on the Rebel works at New Market Heights was one of the most stubborn of the war, with the bulk of the fighting being done by black troops, who sustained more than 50 percent casualties in their determined assault upon the Confederate fortifications. The black troops were asked to take a strong position protected in the front by two lines of abatis and one of palisades, in the rear of which the Texans of Gregg's Brigade poured out a deadly hailstorm of bullets, cutting down the black soldiers by the score.

As the initial attack stalled at the abatis in front of the Confederate works,

Grave of Sergeant Milton M. Holland, USA

Colonel Draper tried to get the men to continue the charge but his orders could not be heard over the roar of the battle. All along the lines, white officers were being shot down. This was particularly true in the 5th U.S.C.T. Lieutenant Colonel Shirtliff, commander of the 5th, was mortally wounded. At this critical point in the battle, black soldiers rose from the ranks to replace the white officers who had been killed or wounded. When all of the white officers of company C had been shot down, Sergeant Milton M. Holland stepped forward and took command of that company. Rallying his men, Sergeant Holland gallantly led them forward against the Confederate works.

Inspired by the courage of men like Sergeant Milton Holland, the black soldiers surged forward and overwhelmed the Rebel works. As they closed with their adversaries and engaged in hand-to-hand combat, no quarter was expected from the Rebels and none was given. In the end, it was the Rebels who broke and ran from the field. Sergeant Milton Holland proved that he was, in every way, a man worthy of the freedom that Bird Holland had given to him.

Once in command of Company C, Sergeant Holland was wounded in the attack but refused to relinquish his command or leave the field. General Butler was so impressed with Sergeant Holland's performance that the general recommended Sergeant Holland for promotion to captain. Because of his color, however, Holland was refused a commission by the War Department. General Butler later said of Sergeant Holland: "Had it been within my power, I would have conferred upon him in view of it, a brigadier-generalship for gallantry on the field."

Milton Holland was mustered out of the service on September 20, 1865. After the war, Holland served for a time as the chief of the collections division of the Sixth Auditor's office in Washington, D.C. In the 1890s, Holland founded Alpha Insurance Company in Washington, D.C., one of the first black owned insurance companies in the nation.

Milton M. Holland died of a heart attack on May 15, 1910. He is buried in the Arlington National Cemetery at Arlington, Virginia.

Corporal Miles James, USA

36th U.S. Colored Troops

Miles James was born in 1829 at Princess Anne County, Virginia. Prior to his enlistment, James stated that his occupation was that of a farmer. He enlisted in Company B, 36th U.S. Colored Troops at Portsmouth, Virginia.

Corporal James is one of the thirteen African Americans who earned the Medal of Honor on September 29, 1864, at the battle of New Market Heights (Chapin's Farm). Corporal James' Medal of Honor citation reads as follows:

> Having had his arm mutilated, making immediate amputation necessary, he loaded and discharged his piece with one hand and urged his men forward; this within 30 yards of the enemy works.

Although seriously wounded, having lost his left arm, Sergeant James did not want to be sent home. His people were not yet free and his job was not yet done. He sent a letter to General A. G. Draper requesting he be allowed to stay in the army. General Draper wrote the following letter, which is now in Miles James' service records in the National Archives in Washington D.C.

> Sergeant Miles James, Co. B, 36th U.S.C.T. writes me from your hospital to urge that he be permitted to remain in the service. He lost his left arm in the charge upon New Market Heights, September 29, 1864. If it be possible, I would most respectfully urge that his request be granted. He was made a Sergeant and awarded a silver medal by Major General Benjamin Butler, for gallant conduct. He is one of the bravest men I ever saw; and is in every respect a model soldier. He is worth more with a single arm, than half a dozen ordinary men. Being a Sergeant he will have very little occasion as a file closer to use a musket. He could be a Sergeant of my Provost-Guard, and could do full duty in many ways. If consistent with your views of duty, I would be greatly obliged if you can make it convenient for him to return to his Regiment.

General Draper's request was granted and Sergeant James was returned to duty with a Sergeant's sword rather than a musket. He served until October 13, 1865, when he was discharged for disability.

Miles James died on August 28, 1871. He is buried at an unknown cemetery in Norfolk County, Virginia.

1st Sergeant Alexander Kelly, USA

6th U.S. Colored Troops

Alexander Kelly was born on April 7, 1840, at Saltsburg, Indiana County, Pennsylvania. Kelly was 23 years old at the time of entering the Army and stated that his occupation was a coal miner. He enlisted in the Army at Allegheny, Pennsylvania, as a substitute for a Joseph Kelly, who is identified as an African American. Alexander Kelly was assigned to Company F, 6th U.S. Colored Troops.

Kelly was appointed 1st Sergeant on September 3, 1863, at Camp William Penn. He was returned to the rank of private on April 29, 1864, at Camp Hamilton, Virginia, but was subsequently reinstated to his former rank of sergeant.

Sergeant Kelly is one of the thirteen African Americans who earned the Medal of Honor on September 29, 1864, at the battle of New Market Heights (Chapin's Farm). When the black soldiers charged the Confederate works at New Market Heights, Gregg's Brigade of Texans responded with an intense musket and cannon fire which decimated the oncoming troops. Most of the white officers leading the black soldiers were either killed or wounded and confusion began to threaten the advance. At the first line of abatis, the color bearer of the 6th U.S. Colored Troops was shot down and the attack began to falter. At this critical point, Sergeant Kelly grabbed the flag from the ground, making himself a conspicuous target for the Rebel marksmen. Under intense fire, Sergeant Kelly rallied his company and led it forward over the Rebel works. Sergeant Kelly's citation for the Medal of Honor reads as follows: "Gallantly seized the colors, which had fallen near the enemy's lines of abatis, raised them and rallied the men at a time of confusion and in a place of the greatest danger."

Sergeant Kelly was returned to the rank of private on July 12, 1865, for censoring his commanding officer. Kelly's training and leadership were too valuable for the Army to waste, however, and he was restored to the rank of sergeant on August 1, 1865.

Alexander Kelly died on June 19, 1907. He is buried at St. Peters Cemetery, Pittsburgh, Pennsylvania.

Landsman John Henry Lawson, USN

U.S.S. Hartford

John H. Lawson was born June 16, 1837, at Philadelphia, Pennsylvania. When the call went out for men to serve in the Union Navy, Lawson was one of the first black Pennsylvanians to volunteer. Upon his enlistment, he was given the rank of Landsman, which is the rank given to new and inexperienced sailors, and was assigned to serve aboard the U.S.S. *Hartford*, Rear Admiral David G. Farragut's flagship.

Lawson was a short and stocky man. His size made him ideally suited for duty on the shell whip on the berth deck just below the main gun stations. The shell whip was a device that raised full powder boxes to the gun deck and lowered empty powder boxes to the deck below, where they were filled by powder boys. Keeping the shell whip in operation during a battle was hard work. Run exclusively on the muscle power and sweat of six men, the operation of the shell whip was essential for the guns to keep firing.

Landsman Lawson saw action aboard the *Hartford* during the capture of New Orleans, and the bombardment of Vicksburg and Port Hudson. It was at the battle of Mobile Bay, however, that Lawson earned the Medal of Honor.

On the morning of August 5, 1864, the *Hartford* led a fleet of 14 Union ships, past the blazing guns of forts Gaines, Morgan and Powell, into Mobile Bay. No sooner had the *Hartford* run the gauntlet of the forts than the Confederate ram, *Tennessee*, attacked. The *Hartford* responded with her nine-inch smooth-bore guns and a full fledged naval battle was in progress.

Landsman John Henry Lawson, USN

Below the gun deck, Landsman John Lawson, Landsman Wilson Brown and four other sailors, sweat pouring down their bodies, were tugging with all their might on the shell whip. Suddenly, an enemy shell exploded in the midst of the six man crew. Four of the crewmen were killed instantly. Lawson was violently thrown against the bulkhead of the ship. Landsman Brown was knocked off the berth deck and was thrown through the hatchway to the lower deck, where he was knocked unconscious.

Lawson lay slumped against the bulkhead, stunned by the blast. As he began to gather his wits about him, he noticed his left leg felt numb. Lawson tried to stand but was unable to get up. He could not see his leg and for a moment he thought it had been shot off. As his head continued to clear, he was relieved to find that he was sitting on his leg. A medic came onto the scene and found Landsman Lawson the only man alive on the deck. Lawson's leg was bleeding from a deep shrapnel wound. When he tried to take Lawson below for treatment, Lawson refused, saying, "The guns must be served first!" With that remark, Lawson returned to his duties at the shell whip. Ignoring the pain and the shells bursting around him, Lawson concentrated on doing his duty.

Wilson Brown regained consciousness, crawling out from under the body of a dead man who had fallen on top of him. He promptly returned to the shell whip on the berth deck. For the remainder of the battle, which lasted several hours, Lawson and Wilson pulled the whip. This was the only means of supplying the gun crew above.

Both Lawson and Brown were awarded the Medal of Honor for their valor aboard the U.S.S. *Hartford* during the battle of Mobile Bay. They were two of the six African Americans who earned the Navy Medal of Honor during the Civil War.

After his discharge in 1864, Lawson worked as a barber and a night watchman for a firehouse. John Henry Lawson died May 3, 1919, at Philadelphia, Pennsylvania. He is buried at the Mount Peace Cemetery at Camden, New Jersey.

Engineer's Cook James Mifflin, USN

U.S.S. Brooklyn

James Mifflin was born in 1839 at Richmond, Richmond County, Virginia. On April 2, 1864, Mifflin enlisted in the U.S. Navy in Virginia.

Prior to his enlistment, Mifflin indicated his occupation as a cook. He was assigned to serve as Engineer's Cook aboard the U.S.S. *Brooklyn*.

Cook James Mifflin was one of the four African Americans to earn the Medal of Honor on August 5, 1864, at the Battle of Mobile Bay. For further details concerning the Battle of Mobile Bay, see the record of Landsman John Lawson. Mifflin's citation reads as follows:

> On board the U.S.S. *Brooklyn* during successful attacks against Fort Morgan, rebel gunboats and the ram *Tennessee* in Mobile Bay on August 5, 1864. Stationed in the immediate vicinity of the shell whips, which were twice cleared of men by bursting shells, Mifflin remained steadfast at his post and performed his duties in the powder division throughout the furious action, which resulted in the surrender of the prize rebel ram *Tennessee* and in the damaging and destruction of the batteries of Fort Morgan.

James Mifflin's medal was approved on December 31, 1864, and would have been awarded sometime in early 1865. After receiving the Medal of Honor, James Miffin simply disappears into history. Nothing more is known about his life, his family, his death or the place of his burial.

Seaman Joachim Pease, USN
U.S.S. Kersarge

Joachim Pease was born in 1842 at Long Island, New York. When the war broke out, Pease, a freeman, enlisted in the U.S. Navy to fight. He wanted to fight to preserve his country and to free his race from the hated institution of slavery. He enlisted at New York City, New York, and was assigned to the U.S.S. *Kersarge.*

Seaman Pease earned the Medal of Honor on June 19, 1864, off the coast of Cherbourg, France, when the U.S.S. *Kersarge* caught, fought and sunk the C.S.S. *Alabama,* the most successful of the Confederate commerce raiders. His citation reads as follows:

> Served as a seaman aboard the U.S.S. *Kersarge* when she destroyed the *Alabama* off Cherbourge France, June 19, 1864. Acting as loader on the No. 2 gun during this bitter engagement, Pease exhibited marked coolness and good conduct

and was highly recommended by the divisional officer for gallantry under fire.

The fight with the C.S.S. *Alabama* lasted only for about an hour and a half. During that time, Seaman Pease worked his gun with cool efficiency and precision. Every four or five minutes, the No. 2 gun fired its deadly shells at the Confederate ship. After each shot, Seaman James H. Lee would cool the gun with his sponge and Pease would call for more powder, and reload the gun. As the battle thundered all around them, and men were wounded and killed, Pease and Lee worked together with a rhythm that kept the No. 2 gun firing. At times, Lee barely had time to cool the gun before it would be fired again.

When a Confederate shell landed within a few feet of the No. 2 gun, both Pease and Lee were showered with shrapnel and knocked to the deck. Both men were stunned but otherwise unhurt. In an instant Pease was on his feet calling for powder. "We'll show them huh, Jim?" Pease called to his sponger as they sent another shell hurling back at the *Alabama*, just to show they weren't dead yet. Shortly thereafter, the Confederate flag was lowered and a white flag raised. Within minutes after that, the *Alabama* sank to the bottom of the sea. She would be sinking no more Union merchant ships.

Ultimately, the battle between the C.S.S. *Alabama* and the U.S.S. *Kersarge* was a lopsided affair. The professionalism and dedication of the crew of the *Kersarge* were demonstrated by the fact that, while the gunners of the *Alabama* fired 370 rounds at the *Kersarge,* only 28 of the Rebel shots actually found their mark. On the other hand the gunners of the *Kersarge* fired just 173 shells at the *Alabama,* almost all of which hit the Rebel raider.

Among those who had performed with excellence in the engagement was Seaman Joachim Pease. Acting Master David H. Sumner, his superior officer, personally congratulated Pease, saying, "You sustained your reputation as one of the best men on the ship."

Seaman Joachim Pease and his sponger, Seaman James H. Lee, were both awarded the Medal of Honor for their valor in this engagement.

1st Sergeant Robert A. Pinn, USA

5th U.S. Colored Troops

Robert A. Pinn was born on March 1, 1843, at Stark County, Ohio. Pinn's father, William, had been a slave in Fauquier County, Virginia.

In 1816, William Pinn escaped from his master, fleeing west to Steubenville, Ohio. Three years later, William moved to Stark County where he lived for the rest of his life. William Pinn and his wife, Zilphia (Broxon) Pinn, had ten children of which Robert was the sixth. When the war broke out Robert Pinn was anxious to join in the fight against slavery, but found himself excluded due to his race. Unwilling to be denied, Robert Pinn entered the service of his country as an aid to Frederick T. Hurxthal, the surgeon of the 19th Ohio Infantry. At the Battle of Shiloh, Tennessee, Pinn, although technically a noncombatant, took up a musket and fought in the battle. Thereafter, whenever the 19th Ohio was engaged, Pinn took his position in the line and earned a reputation for bravery.

In 1863, with acceptance of colored troops into the Union Army, Pinn enlisted at Massillion, Ohio, in Company I, 5th U.S. Colored Troops. He was 21 years old at the time of his enlistment and listed his occupation as a farmer. Pinn was promoted to sergeant October 18, 1863, and was promoted to first sergeant September 1, 1864.

Sergeant Pinn earned the Medal of Honor on September 29, 1864, for his heroism at the Battle of New Market Heights, Virginia, also known as Chapin's Farm. Sergeant Pinn's citation reads as follows: "Took command of his company after all the officers had been killed or wounded and gallantly led it in battle."

At the Battle of New Market Heights, Sergeant Pinn took command of Company I after all of the officers had been killed or wounded. Leading the Company forward, Sergeant Pinn was himself wounded three times—first, in the left thigh, second, in his left arm and third, in his right shoulder. Despite the seriousness of his wounds, Sergeant Pinn refused to leave the field. He detailed two men from his command to carry him forward at the head of the Company throughout the battle.

Pinn's military service records at the National Archives in Washington, D.C., establish the following: Sergeant Pinn was wounded at Fort Gilmer, Virginia, on September 29, 1864, and sent to hospital at Portsmouth Grove, Rhode Island. Sergeant Pinn was mustered out of the Army on September 20, 1865, at Carolina City, North Carolina.

After the war, Pinn returned to Stark County where he engaged in a teaming and contracting business. In 1867, he married Emily J. Manzilla of Mahoning County, Ohio. Pinn sold his business and, from 1874 to 1877, he attended Oberlin College. He then studied the law under R.H. Folger of Massillion, Ohio. On April 3, 1879, Pinn was admitted to the

Stark County Bar. He practiced law and served as the United States Pension Attorney in that area. Pinn was also active in the GAR (Grand Army of the Republic) and served as a member of the Stark County Soldiers Relief Commission, which provided relief to indigent soldiers and their families.

Robert A. Pinn died on January 1, 1911, at Massillion, Ohio. Out of respect for their fellow attorney, the Star County Court of Common Pleas halted hearings and the entire bar attended his funeral. Pinn is buried at the City Cemetery, Massillion, Ohio.

1st Sergeant Edward Ratcliff, USA

38th U.S. Colored Troops

Edward Ratcliff was born on March 10, 1835, at James County, Virginia. On January 28, 1864, he enlisted as a private in Company C, 38th U.S. Colored Troops, at Yorktown, Virginia. Private Ratcliff was promoted to 1st Sergeant on February 1, 1864, when his company was mustered into service.

Sergeant Radcliff is one of the thirteen African Americans who earned the Medal of Honor on September 29, 1864, at the Battle of New Market Heights (Chapin's Farm). The attack on the Rebel works at New Market Heights was one of the most stubborn of the war, with the bulk of the fighting being done by black troops, who sustained more than 50 percent casualties in the determined charge. The black troops had been asked to take a strong position, protected in the front by two lines of abatis and one line of palisades, and in the rear of which the Texans of Gregg's Brigade poured out a deadly hailstorm of bullets.

As the initial attack stalled at the abatis in front of the Confederate works, Colonel Draper tried to get the men to continue the charge, but his orders could not be heard over the roar of the battle. All along the lines, white officers were being shot down. At this critical point in the battle, black soldiers rose from the ranks to replace the white officers who had been killed or wounded. Sergeant Edward Ratcliff took command of Company D, after all of its officers had been killed or wounded, and gallantly led his men forward against the enemy works.

Inspired by the courage and example of such men as Sergeant Ratcliff, the black soldiers surged forward and took the Rebel works. The first to enter the works were Sergeant James H. Harris, Sergeant Edward Ratcliff and Private William H. Barnes of the 38th U.S.C.T. and Private James Gardiner of the 36th U.S.C.T. Their comrades followed them into the Rebel works, where they met the enemy face to face, and black men with arms of iron fought Southern white solders hand to hand with desperate valor. In the end, it was those who held the philosophy that black men were inferior and fit only to be the slaves of other men that were driven from the field.

On December 24, 1864, Sergeant Ratcliff was promoted to sergeant-major and transferred to the regimental staff. Ratcliff was reduced in rank from sergeant-major to 1st sergeant on August 31, 1865.

Edward Ratcliff died on March 10, 1915, at Nelson, Virginia. He is buried at Chescake Cemetery Naval Station, Lackey, Virginia.

Color Sergeant
Andrew Jackson Smith, USA

55th Massachusetts Infantry

Andrew Jackson Smith was born around September 3, 1842. Fathered by his wealthy slave owner, Elijah Smith, and birthed by a slave named Susan, Andy Smith was born a slave. When he was ten years old, he was assigned by his owner to run a ferry transporting people and supplies across the Cumberland River. Andy became known as a skilled boatman and continued his craft for nearly eight years.

When the war started, Andy's father and owner, Elijah Smith, had been quick to enlist in the Confederacy. When Elijah returned home on leave after a year's absence, he planned, as was the custom of many Confederate officers, to take his slave, Andy, back with him. Andy, who was nineteen at the time, overheard the plans and decided to run away.

On the river, Andy had learned its currents and its people. Furthermore, he heard the talk about the War, and he saw the Yankee ships, the steamers, the paddle wheels, and the ironclads. He was aware that the ships and the U.S. troops were stationed up the river at Smithland, where the Cumberland and the Ohio Rivers converged.

Smithland was being used as a strategic military outpost by the U.S. troops, who could control the movement on the Ohio, and access to the

Mississippi River from the north and access to the Cumberland from the east.

Andy Smith and another slave decided to run to Smithland when they overheard their owners plotting to take them to serve the Confederacy. They walked the nearly 25 miles in freezing rain so cold that their soaked clothes froze to their bodies. They had to wait until daylight to present themselves to the 41st Illinois guards. They were admitted into the camp and given warm clothes and provided hot food. Andy later described joining the 41st Illinois as "falling in."

When the companies at Smithland rejoined the rest of the 41st Illinois Regiment at Paducah, Kentucky, Andy became a servant to Major John Warner in order to remain under the protection of the military. Major Warner and Andy had agreed that, should Warner fall in battle, Andy would take his belongings to his home in Clinton, Illinois. The Major Warner wrote home advising his family of this arrangement.

The 41st Illinois Volunteer Regiment moved on to Fort Henry for battle. The battle was short but successful. The fort fell and they captured Confederate General Lloyd Tillingham.

The 41st Illinois then moved on to Fort Donelson where the unit encountered fierce resistance and lost over 200 men. On March 10, 1862, the 41st Regiment traveled to Pittsburg Landing (Shiloh). Prior to this battle, Major Warner had asked Andy Smith to observe him, and if he should fall, he wanted Andy to bring him water.

During the battle, the Major Warner had his mount shot from under him. When he got up, there was Andy with another mount. Shortly afterwards when the second mount was killed, Andy caught a Confederate horse and gave it to the major. Andy asked if he could stay close to the battlefield. Before he could walk away, he was struck by a spent minié ball that entered his left temple, rolled just under the skin, and stopped in the middle of his forehead. As Andy laid his head upon the regimental surgeon's bloody apron, the surgeon removed the ball after which he pulled a sponge through the wound to cleanse it. Andy carried the scar to his grave seventy years later.

John Warner returned to Clinton, Illinois, as a colonel in November of 1862, along with Andy, who continued to serve him. Andy was in Clinton, Illinois, when he heard the news that President Lincoln had acquiesced and permitted black troops to fight for their freedom. Andy Smith left the safety of a free state to enroll in the 54th Massachusetts Colored Volunteers. Massachusetts Governor John Andrew had requested

1000 black men, and he got nearly 2,000 so quickly that he had to disband the 55th Massachusetts regulars to handle the overflow. The 55th was renamed to accommodate the colored recruits.

Andy Smith and 55 other Illinois volunteers were mustered in the 55th Massachusetts Colored Volunteers. Andy mustered into Company "B" on May 16, 1863. After the 54th Massachusetts Volunteer Regiment's engagement at Fort Wagner, South Carolina, on July 18, 1863, the 54th and the 55th fought five military engagements together over the next three years. They fought both on and off the battlefield. They fought and won the battle for equal pay with white soldiers. But in order to receive his pay, a black soldier was required to nod his head (yes) when asked if he was free in 1861. Andy refused to nod and lie about his status prior to 1861 in order to receive his pay.

Andy Smith was fortunate that he did not receive any other serious wounds during his 55th Massachusetts enlistment, even though he served in the color bearer unit. He was always in the thick of battle and volunteered for many raids among the islands along the South Carolina and Georgia coasts.

Andy won his distinction at the Battle of Honey Hill, South Carolina, when the flag bearer was blown to bits by an exploding shell. Andy caught the falling color sergeant, Robert King, with one hand and snatched the flag with the other. Lieutenant Ellsworth, who was the commander at the time, screamed at Smith, "For God's sake, save the flag!" Smith carried the colors during the rest of the battle.

As he was leaving the field at Honey Hill, the regimental color sergeant was wounded, and Andy left the field of battle bearing both flags. Had his actions been properly recorded that day, he certainly would have been rewarded with the Medal of Honor for his bravery under fire.

The regimental commander, Colonel Hartwell, was severely wounded and carried from battle early in the fighting. He was forced to complete his battle report at his home while recuperating from his wounds. Had the colonel been present for the remainder of the battle, he might have reacted differently to Andy's bravery.

Sergeant Smith's Medal of Honor citation reads as follows:

> Corporal Andrew Jackson Smith, of Clinton, Illinois, a member of the 55th Massachusetts Volunteer Infantry, distinguished himself on 30 November 1864 by saving his regimental colors, after the color bearer was killed during a bloody charge called the Battle of Honey Hill, South Carolina. In the late afternoon, as the 55th Regiment pursued

enemy skirmishers and conducted a running fight, they ran into a swampy area backed by a rise where the Confederate Army awaited. The surrounding woods and thick underbrush impeded infantry movement and artillery support. The 55th and 54th regiments formed columns to advance on the enemy position in a flanking movement. As the Confederates repelled other units, the 55th and 54th regiments continued to move into flanking positions. Forced into a narrow gorge crossing a swamp in the face of the enemy position, the 55th's Color-Sergeant was killed by an exploding shell, and Corporal Smith took the Regimental Colors from his hand and carried them through heavy grape and canister fire. Although half of the officers and a third of the enlisted men engaged in the fight were killed or wounded, Corporal Smith continued to expose himself to enemy fire by carrying the colors throughout the battle. Through his actions, the Regimental Colors of the 55th Infantry Regiment were not lost to the enemy. Corporal Andrew Jackson Smith's extraordinary valor in the face of deadly enemy fire is in keeping with the highest traditions of military service and reflect great credit upon him, the 55th Regiment, and the United States Army.

Andy was promoted to Color Sergeant soon after the battle. The 55th Massachusetts Colored remained in the area and was later detailed as provost guard at Orangeburg, South Carolina. Andy received his final discharge at Mt. Pleasant, South Carolina, on August 29, 1865, and was sent to Boston on the steamer *Karnac* for his formal mustering out.

After the war, Andy went back to Clinton, Illinois, for a short period. He later returned to Eddyville, Kentucky, where he used his mustering out pay to buy land.

Dr. Burt G. Wilder, who was the regimental surgeon for the 55th Massachusetts, began a lifelong correspondence with Andy Smith in hopes of securing the cherished Medal of Honor for Andy's bravery at Honey Hill. So many of the officers were wounded and taken from the battlefield that the battle was never fully documented and Andy's heroics could not be certified.

On January 16, 2001, during the same ceremony in which Theodore Roosevelt was awarded the Medal of Honor, President Clinton also awarded a Medal of Honor to Andrew Jackson Smith. The awarding of Smith's medal set a record for the longest period between a soldier's service and recognition of it with the highest U.S. military honor.

Private Charles Veal, USA

4th U.S. Colored Troops

Charles Veal was born in 1838 at Portsmouth, Portsmouth County, Virginia. At the time of his enlistment, Veal stated that he was 28 years old and gave his occupation as a fireman. He entered the army as a private in Company D, 4th U.S. Colored Infantry, at Baltimore, Maryland. Veal was promoted to corporal on August 28, 1863.

Corporal Veal earned the Medal of Honor on September 29, 1864, at New Market Heights (Chapin's Farm), Virginia. When the 4th U.S.C.T. advanced against the Confederate works that morning, Sergeant Hilton was one of the color sergeants and was carrying the national colors. The colored troops marched into a firestorm of shot, shell and musket fire. Men fell on all sides, swept down by the intense Confederate fire.

When the color bearer carrying the regimental colors was shot down, Sergeant Hilton took up the colors, carrying both flags forward. As the Confederate fire swept the field, Sergeant Hilton was shot through the leg. As he fell, he held up the flags and cried out, "Boys, save the colors!" Before they could touch the ground, the flags were taken by Private Veal and Sergeant Fleetwood, who courageously bore them forward. Sergeant Hilton, Private Veal and Sergeant Fleetwood all earned the Medal of Honor that day.

Concerning the engagement, Sergeant Christian Fleetwood later said:

> I have never been able to understand how Veal and I lived under such a hail of bullets, unless it was because we were both such little fellows. I think I weighed then about 125 pounds and Veal about the same. We did not get a scratch. A bullet passed between my legs, cutting my boot leg trousers and even my stockings without breaking the skin.

Corporal Veal was promoted to the rank of Sergeant on November 12, 1864.

Charles Veal died on July 27, 1872 at Hampton, Virginia. He is buried at the Hampton National Cemetery, Hampton, Virginia.

Chapter 2

The Indian Wars (1866–1890)

By the end of the Civil War, the War Department had seen the value of black soldiers. By an act passed on July 28, 1866, Congress authorized the creation of six African American regiments to serve in the regular Army. Four of these regiments were to be infantry regiments and two were to be cavalry regiments. The four infantry regiments, the 38th, 39th, 40th and 41st U.S. Infantry, were quickly consolidated into two regiments, the 24th and 25th U.S. Infantry, which were stationed in Texas until 1880. The 24th Infantry was then transferred to Indian Territory (Oklahoma) and the 25th was sent to South Dakota.

The two cavalry regiments became the 9th and 10th U.S. Cavalry, the famous "buffalo soldiers" who played an important role in opening the west. For 24 years the 9th and 10th Cavalry campaigned on the Great Plains, along the Rio Grande, in New Mexico, Arizona, Colorado and the Dakotas.

The new black units made up a substantial part of the post Civil War regular Army. The two infantry regiments made up approximately 10 percent of the twenty-five regiments in the service. The 9th and 10th Cavalry made up 20 percent of the ten cavalry regiments. By 1870 there were approximately 30,000 soldiers in the Army. Black soldiers comprised 2,700 of these men.

These "buffalo soldiers" fought Indians, bandits, bootleggers, cattle thieves, gun runners and Mexican revolutionaries. They performed their duties with honor and distinction over some of the most forbidding terrain and extremes of climate the United States has to offer.

While the life of a black trooper was difficult, the Army offered to the soldiers and their non-commissioned officers an opportunity for advancement and at least a partial equality. It began to attract some of the best and brightest African Americans. They included men like Sergeant Joseph Moore of the 9th Cavalry, who led a drive to buy John Brown's Fort at Harpers Ferry, West Virginia, and preserve it as a historical site; Fort Robinson's intelligent and multitalented telegraph operator and post librarian, Private C.D. Dillard; and Medal of Honor recipient Edward L. Baker, Jr., who spoke both French and Spanish fluently and dabbled in Russian and Chinese.

Nor was it possible to teach men a sense of duty and honor and expect them to remain subservient to prejudice and injustice. Individually and collectively, black soldiers with a well-earned sense of pride began to stand up for themselves. Company E, of the 9th U.S. Cavalry, led by Sergeant Harrison Bradford, mutinied against its officers when Lieutenant Edward Heyl brutalized three enlisted men by hanging them by their wrists from a tree for a trivial infraction, and then beating one of the men with his sword for seeking to ease his pain by putting his feet on a stump. The courageous Sergeant Bradford was killed and Lieutenant Heyl badly wounded before the matter was sorted out. On another occasion, Sergeant John Jackson killed a white soldier who had threatened his life.

Another distinct group of African Americans who earned the Medal of Honor during the Indian Wars were the Negro Seminole Indian scouts. The ancestors of these men had fled slavery by fleeing into south Florida, where they found refuge among the Seminole Indians. The runaway slaves found acceptance among the Seminole and were assimilated into the tribe. Interestingly, the word "Seminole" is a Creek word meaning "runaway." When the U.S. Government removed the Seminole Indians from Florida, the adopted black members of the tribe went with them. Several of the black Indians, afraid that they would be returned to slavery, fled into Mexico in the early 1850s. By 1870, the situation had changed. A number of Negro Seminole Indians, under Chief John Horse, were interested in returning to the United States now that it no longer tolerated slavery. White officers such as Major Bliss, aware of the service the Negro Seminoles had given to the Mexican Army, encouraged their return and offered them employment as scouts.

On July 4, 1870, the first group of Negro Seminole Indians crossed the Rio Grand to Fort Duncan, Texas, and offered the Army their services as scouts. Their offers were accepted and the Negro Seminole Scouts were organized. This group served with distinction throughout the Indian Wars. The scouts were finally abolished in 1914.

Eighteen African Americans earned the Medal of Honor for their courage in the Indian Wars. These included both ex-slaves and free men as well as four Negro Seminole Scouts. The stories of their valor and courage follow.

Sergeant Thomas Boyne, USA

9th U.S. Cavalry

A native of Prince Georges County, Maryland, Thomas Boyne was born in 1849. He fought in the Civil War as a member of Battery C, 2nd U.S. Colored Light Artillery. He participated in the battles around Richmond, at Wilson's Wharf and City Point, Virginia. After the war, Boyne went west with his unit and was discharged in March 1866 at Brownsville, Texas. Ten months later, Boyne decided to make the Army a career and he reenlisted in the 40th Infantry under the name of Thomas Bowen. Boyne served with the 40th until the regiment was consolidated as the 25th U.S. Infantry. In 1875, he joined Company C, 9th U.S. Cavalry.

Sergeant Boyne was awarded the Medal of Honor for two separate actions against Victorio and his Apache warriors. The first of these actions occurred on May 29, 1879, at Mimbres Mountains, New Mexico. The second action was at the Cuchillo Negro River near Ojo Caliente, New Mexico, on September 27, 1879.

In May 1879, the decision was made to transfer Victorio, Juh and their followers from the reservation at Ojo Caliente back to the reservation at San Carlos. The large Indian reservation at San Carlos was hell on earth. The Apaches simply loathed the remote and barren San Carlos reservation. Owen Wister, who wrote *The Virginian,* claimed that God had not made San Carlos, but, after he had created paradise with its gardens and fruit trees, he left San Carlos as he had found it so that people could see what he had had to work with when he started. According to Wister, San Carlos was the result of a simple recipe: "Take stones and ashes and thorns, some scorpions and rattle-snakes thrown in, dump the outfit on stones real hot, set the United States Army after the Apaches, and you have San Carlos."

Juh and his followers had had enough and submitted to the decision, but Victorio and Warm Springs Apaches made a break from the reservation and headed for the safety of Mexico. On May 25, Captain Charles D. Beyer and 46 enlisted men from companies C and I of the 9th Cavalry were sent from Fort Bayard to intercept the Apaches before they could get to the border.

On May 29th, the troopers found the Apaches on top of one of the Mimbres Mountains, constructing a breastworks for their defense. Captain Beyer sent a small detachment, consisting of Guide Foster and five cavalrymen, to capture the Apaches' herd. The small detachment captured all of the animals—ten horses, two mules and two burros. Captain Beyer formed the rest of his men into a skirmish line and began to ascend the mountain. Victorio raised a white flag and called down that he wanted to talk to the leader of the soldiers. Captain Beyer halted his men, put a white flag on a stick and advanced about 50 yards in front of his line. Victorio, however, would not come down to meet with the Captain, and Captain Beyer was not willing to go into the breastworks to talk to Victorio. When further attempts to negotiate proved fruitless, Captain Beyer again ordered the skirmish line to advance and a battle was commenced.

Captain Beyer described the battle as follows:

> The line kept advancing, the men seeking shelter from tree to tree, and after about a half an hour's sharp fighting, during which the right skirmishers had gotten well around and to the rear of the position held by the Indians, the latter abandoned their works and camp and scattered, my men gaining the position from which they had driven the Indians a few minutes after they retreated. The Indians, being afoot left no trail and could not be pursued.

During the battle, Lieutenant Henry Wright, with a few men, were escorting a wounded soldier to the rear. The troopers were suddenly ambushed by a group of Apaches. The lieutenant's horse was killed and his small command quickly surrounded and cut off. Ever alert, Sergeant Boyne noticed that the Indians had the lieutenant and his men surrounded. With a small detachment of troopers, Sergeant Boyne went charging to the rescue. Under Boyne's direction, the troopers quickly flanked the Indians, who were forced to abandon their prey and flee themselves to avoid being killed or captured.

During the second engagement, Sergeant Boyne was serving with almost two hundred officers and men under Major Albert P. Morrow in an action against their old foe, Victorio and his Apaches. On September 27, 1879, at Cuchillo, New Mexico, the 9th Cavalry confronted the Apache warriors near Ojo Caliente. For two days the Indians and cavalrymen fought a running battle. Sergeant Boyne, though wounded, killed one of three warriors and single-handedly captured a considerable number of the 60 horses and mules that were taken in the battle. For his participation in this fight, Lieutenant Wright recommended Boyne for a Medal of Honor. The recommendation was endorsed by Major Morrow who wrote:

> I have seen him repeatedly in action and in every instance he distinguished himself.... I cannot speak too highly of his conduct.... If ever a soldier ever deserves a Certificate of Merit or a Medal of Honor Sergeant Boyne does and I hope he may be so rewarded.

Sergeant Boyne was awarded the Medal of Honor rather than a Certificate of Merit because the law authorized the Certificate of Merit only for privates and as a sergeant Boyne was not qualified. Thomas Boyne received his Medal of Honor on January 6, 1882. His citation simply reads: "Bravery in action."

Thomas Boyne was discharged from the Army in January 1889 for disability, after completing almost 25 years of service. Sergeant Boyne's health had been failing him for some time. He suffered a severe case of frostbite during the winter of 1884-1885 in Indian Territory (Oklahoma). The last straw came when Sergeant Boyne developed a hernia while supervising a wood gathering detail at Fort Missoula, Montana, in October 1888.

After his discharge from the Army, Boyne was taken in at the U.S. Soldier's Home in Washington, D.C., in 1890. He remained there, associating with his old comrades until his death from consumption on April 21, 1896. Boyne is buried in the Soldier's Home National Cemetery in Washington, D.C.

Sergeant Benjamin Brown

24th U.S. Infantry

Benjamin Brown was born in 1859 in Spotsylvania County, Virginia. He enlisted in the Army in 1880, at Harrisburg, Pennsylvania, and was assigned to Company C, 24th U.S. Infantry.

Sergeant Brown earned the Medal of Honor on February 18, 1890. On that date Sergeant Brown was serving as part of an escort of two non-commissioned officers and nine privates for Major Joseph W. Wham, paymaster, U.S. Army, who was transporting the payroll between forts Grant and Thomas in Arizona. The detail was attacked by a band of robbers who had rolled a large boulder weighing several tons onto the road and set an ambush. Just as the troopers were about to try to move the boulder out of the way a single shot was fired from the ledge of rocks about 50 feet above and behind the troopers. The shot was followed immediately by a volley from what Major Wham estimated was 15 to 20 guns. The troopers had been ambushed by a band of robbers intent on capturing the payroll.

In his report on the incident Major Wham stated, "I am convinced that two members of the escort did little or no fighting and almost immediately left the field, which reduced the number actually engaged to nine." Private Lewis Hamilton, Major Wham's driver, was hit in the first volley. He was shot in the stomach and was of no further use in the battle that followed. Major Wham and the remainder of the escort made their stand and fought in the most courageous and heroic manner. For about thirty minutes a sharp but unequal fight ensued. The troopers had been caught in the open while the robbers were entrenched on a rock ledge above them. The troopers attempted valiantly to defend their charge, but eight of the escort were wounded in the fight. Two of these soldiers were shot twice.

Sergeant Benjamin Brown and several of the soldiers had been caught in the open at the first volley and did the best they could to make a fight from where they were. One by one the privates around Sergeant Brown were hit and went down. Many of them were so severely wounded that they could no longer fight. Using his pistol Sergeant Brown held his ground and tried to protect his men. He was shot in the abdomen and went down. Grabbing a carbine from a wounded trooper who could not fight anymore, Brown continued to fire at the robbers until he was shot a second time. This time Sergeant Brown was shot through both arms and was out of the fight.

Eventually the soldiers were forced to withdraw and did so taking their wounded with them. The payroll was abandoned to the robbers. This led to a number of investigations. Marshall Mead, who conducted a thorough investigation, swore that "I am satisfied a braver or better defense could not have been made under like circumstances, and to have remained longer would have proven a useless sacrifice of life without a vestige of hope to succeed."

Lieutenant Cartwright was assigned to investigate the matter on behalf of the Army. Cartwright gave the matter his full attention until the completion of the trial of the men accused of committing the robbery. In his final report, Lieutenant Cartwright credited Major Wham and the escort for doing all that was possible to protect the payroll. He further stated, "That the escort fought well and bravely is attested to by the bullet marks on the robbery position as well as those on the rock occupied by Major Wham and the soldiers."

Major Wham concluded his own report on the matter by recalling that he had served in the Civil War in the regiment which had been commanded by a certain Colonel Ulysses S. Grant. That regiment had participated in 16 battles and was justly proud of its record, but Wham said, "I never witnessed better courage or better fighting than shown by these Colored soldiers, on May 11, 1889." Major Wham recommended Sergeant Brown and Corporal Isaiah Mays for the Medals of Honor and several of their men for certificates of merit. The recommendations were approved by the War Department and the Medal of Honor was issued to Sergeant Brown on February 19, 1890.

Sergeant Brown recovered from his wounds and remained in the Army until 1904 when while serving at Fort Assinniboine, Montana, Brown suffered a stroke which rendered him unfit for further military service. Sergeant Brown was discharged as being permanently disabled. In 1905 he entered the U.S. Soldier's Home in Washington, D.C., where he remained until his death on September 5, 1910. Sergeant Benjamin Brown is buried in the Soldier's Home National Cemetery in Washington, D.C.

Sergeant John Denny, USA

9th U.S. Cavalry

John Denny was born in 1846 at Big Flats, Chemung County, New York. Denny enlisted in the Army in 1867 at Elmira, New York. At the time of his enlistment, he gave his occupation as laborer. He was assigned to Troop D, 9th U.S. Cavalry.

Sergeant Denny earned the Medal of Honor on September 18, 1879, at Las Animas Canyon, New Mexico. His citation reads, "Removed a wounded comrade, under heavy fire, to a place of safety."

On September 4, 1879, Victorio and his band of Apaches were in the vicinity of Ojo Caliente, with a detachment of the 9th Cavalry, under Captain Ambrose E. Hooker, hot on their trail. Victorio and his band were in desperate need of horses. The cavalry had horses. So the ever clever Victorio decided to solve two of his problems at the same time. A night raid on the company's corral killed eight soldiers and netted 46 horses for the old chief.

By September 14, Victorio's band was being pursued by a civilian posse. Suddenly, near Hillsboro, the Indians turned and attacked their pursuers. Ten of the civilians were killed and the Indians rode off with the scalps of the dead white men and more horses.

On September 16, a small detachment of the 9th Cavalry, under the command of Lieutenant Byron Dawson, came across the Indians' trail and followed it into Las Animas Canyon and they rode right into an ambush. The unfortunate troopers were quickly surrounded and cut off. They would have been wiped out had not another force of the 9th Cavalry, under Captain Beyer, come to their rescue. Victorio was not willing to let his prey go just because help had arrived. All day long, the battle raged between the troopers and the Indians. Captain Beyer's men made several attempts to flank the Indians and relieve Dawson's command, but each time they were bloodily repulsed. The Apaches also made several determined attacks on Dawson's small command, trying to annihilate them before their siege could be broken. Dawson's men, although bloodied, fought for their lives and the Indians were unable to exterminate them as planned.

As night fell, the soldiers' ammunition was almost exhausted and it was determined to withdraw under the cover of darkness. To accomplish the withdrawal, all of the wounded soldiers had to be gathered up and taken with the troopers, since any wounded man left on the field would be tortured to death in the most cruel manner and his body severely mutilated after he died. A private named Freeland had taken a bullet in his leg and lay about 400 yards in front of Beyer's command. The situation was critical, as Freeland was unable to make it back to the command, and every inch on the rocky ground between Freeland and the soldiers was covered by fire from the Indians. Everyone could see that any attempt to go to Private Freeland's assistance would be suicidal.

Suddenly, Sergeant Denny dashed from cover over the fire-swept ground towards his stricken comrade. The Indians responded by sending a hail of deadly lead in the direction of the valiant sergeant. The troopers responded, putting up as much of a covering fire as they could. With bullets whistling past his ears and kicking up dust all around him, Sergeant Denny reached Freeland and helped him to his feet. Now slowed by his wounded comrade, Sergeant Denny started back across the field. Lieutenant Day, who would also earn a Medal of Honor that day, stated that "Soon the fire of the hostiles increased so much that it seemed than no one could pass this rocky space alive." As they neared the troopers' line, Private Freeland's strength gave out. Sergeant Denny called for another soldier to assist him and then, lifting the bulky private onto his shoulders and with the assistance of the other soldier, carried him into the troopers' lines.

The soldiers withdrew in the darkness. Victorio had again won the day. Five enlisted men had been killed, as well as two Indian scouts and one civilian scout. In addition, Victorio had killed or wounded 38 Army horses. The cavalry would be unable to follow him. There was no evidence that the Indians had suffered any casualties.

For fifteen years, Denny's deed went unrecognized by the Army. With the help of Lieutenant Day and fellow troopers, Lyman and Jackson, a request for a medal was made for Private Denny. According to Jackson, troopers were still talking about Denny's gallant action in 1894, fifteen years after the event. Sergeant Denny's Medal of Honor was approved and issued on November 27, 1894. In January 1895, Colonel James Biddle, the 9th Cavalry's commander, presented the Medal of Honor to Private Denny.

Denny remained in the Army until 1897, when he retired with 30 years of service as a corporal. Upon his retirement, he settled in Baltimore, Maryland. As his health failed, Denny was admitted to the U.S. Soldier's Home in Washington, D.C., where he died on November 28, 1901. At the time of his death, Denny owned a Medal of Honor, a silver watch and sixty-eight cents. John Denny is buried at the Soldier's Home National Cemetery in Washington, D.C.

Private Pompey Factor, USA

Indian Scouts

Pompey Factor was born in 1849 in Arkansas. Pompey Factor was twenty-one years old when he joined the Army as a scout. He was among the first to enlist in the Seminole Indian Scouts in August 1870 at Fort Duncan, Texas.

Private Factor earned the Medal of Honor on April 25, 1875, at the

Pecos River, Texas. His simple citation reads as follows: "With three others he participated in a charge against 25 hostiles while on a scouting patrol."

Lieutenant John Lapham Bullis was the commander of the Seminole Negro Scouts. Bullis was a brave, tough, unconventional soldier who had served as a captain in the 118th U.S. Colored Troops. Between 1873 and 1881, Bullis received four citations for valor in battle. The scouts quickly came to admire and respect their leader. Scout Joseph Philips testified that Bullis shared the dangers and deprivations of campaigning against the Indians. "That fella suffer just like we all did out in the woods. He was a good man. He was an Indian fighter. He was tough." Lieutenant Bullis led his men from the front and by his example. Again, as Scout Philips remembered, "He did not stand and say 'Go yonder'; he would say, 'Come on, boys, let's go get them.'"

Bullis became a sort of war chief among the scouts and their families. His men expected him to examine and approve each newborn in the Seminole Negro camp. Bullis even performed a marriage ceremony for scout James Perryman and Teresita, the daughter of a Lipan chief who had been captured during a raid into Mexico in 1873.

In a battle on the Pecos River in Texas on April 25, 1875, Trumpeter Isaac Payne, Sergeant John Ward, and Private Pompey Factor were cited for "gallantry in action" against Indians. Lieutenant John Lapham Bullis and the three scouts left Fort Clark on April 16 on a mission to locate a band of Indians who had stolen about 75 horses.

On the 25th, the scouts came across the trail they had been seeking. It was a large trail, which Lieutenant Bullis estimated to have been made by 75 horses or more. The scouts followed the trail and soon came upon the party of Indians, who were in the process of crossing the Pecos River. The scouts quickly found favorable ground and opened the fight. For about three quarters of an hour, the scouts were able to hold their own against the superior numbers, during which time they killed three of the Indians and wounded a fourth.

The four soldiers bravely held their ground, but were outnumbered and outgunned. They were finally forced to withdraw when they noticed a group of Indians moving to cut them off from their horses. Lieutenant Bullis, Sergeant Ward, Private Factor and Trumpeter Payne retreated to where they had tied their horses; the scouts mounted their horses and were on their way out of the trap. Lieutenant Bullis, however, lost his horse in the confusion. The lieutenant was able to attract Sergeant Ward's attention. Sergeant Ward turned his horse around and

Lieutenant Bullis was able to mount behind him and they made good their escape.

Lieutenant Bullis described Sergeant John Ward, Trumpeter Isaac Payne and Private Pompey Factor as "brave and trustworthy" and stated that each was worthy of a medal.

Private Factor deserted from the Army on January 1, 1877, the same day that fellow scout, Adam Paine, was killed by a deputy sheriff. According to Kenneth W. Porter, a leading authority on the Seminole Indian scouts, "Five scouts and former scouts, including Pompey Factor, were so exasperated by this second killing (of a Seminole Negro Indian by whites) within a year — the third in less than two years— that they washed the dust of Texas from their horses' hooves in the waters of the Rio Grande." They entered Mexico and fought Indians for the Mexican Government.

Pompey Factor returned from Mexico and surrendered to the Army on May 25, 1879. The Army pardoned him and returned him to duty, without a trial, on the condition that he would make up the time lost by his desertion. Private Factor's last enlistment ended in 1880. After leaving the Army, Factor took up farming in Musquiz, Mexico, and Brackettville, Texas.

In his late seventies and penniless, Pompey Factor sought an Army pension. His pension request was denied, as the Army claimed it had no records that Pompey Factor had ever served as a scout. Even Factor's empty case that had contained his Medal of Honor was not considered sufficient evidence.

When Pompey Factor died on March 28, 1928, at Brackettville, Texas, a friend paid his funeral expenses of $86.40 because Factor literally had no money. He is buried in the Seminole Indian Scout Cemetery, Brackettville, Texas.

Corporal Clinton Greaves, USA

9th U.S. Cavalry

Clinton Greaves was born on August 12, 1855, in Madison County, Virginia, on the eastern slopes of the Blue Ridge Mountains. Greaves moved from there to Prince George's County, Maryland, where he lived on the outskirts of Washington, D.C. Greaves worked as a laborer in

Prince Georges County before he enlisted in Company C, 9th U.S. Cavalry, in November 1872 at the age of 22.

In January 1877, a party of 40 to 50 Chiricaua Apaches had jumped the reservation and went on the warpath. The Apaches fought a battle with a detachment of the 6th U.S. Cavalry, which had been sent to capture them in Arizona, but the Apaches escaped and were believed to have moved eastward into New Mexico.

Lieutenant Henry H. Wright, with five buffalo soldiers of Company C, 9th U.S. Cavalry, and three Navaho scouts, were dispatched from Fort Bayard to search for the renegades. The Indian camp was discovered in the Florida Mountains on January 24, 1877. The warriors outnumbered his small command by two to one, so Lieutenant Wright did not attack, but neither did he retreat. He rode his small command straight into the Apache camp and called for a parley with the chiefs. Lieutenant Wright tried to convince the Apaches to put down their weapons and surrender. The Apaches, however, seeing that they had the troopers outnumbered, were not willing to surrender and go back to the reservation. Half an hour of negotiations proved futile. The Apaches used the time to have the women and children slip quietly out of the camp, and 18 warriors moved forward to surround the small command.

Lieutenant Wright ordered his men to push through the warriors surrounding the troopers, and a fierce fight at close quarters broke out. Weapons were fired and then used as clubs in the hand-to-hand fighting. The outnumbered troopers were in danger of being overwhelmed. Corporal Clinton Greaves fought like a cornered lion. Greaves fired his carbine until it was empty and then, swinging it like a club, he bashed a gap through the swarming Apaches, allowing his comrades to break free. The Apaches got the worst of this fight. With five dead and several others wounded, the Indians decided they had had enough and left the field to the nine troopers.

Lieutenant Wright recommended that privates Richard Epps, Dick Mackadoo, John Adams and Navaho Scout Jose Chaves receive Certificates of Merit for their bravery in the action. Lieutenant Wright recommended Corporal Clinton Greaves for both a Certificate of Merit and the Medal of Honor for his courage and fighting spirit, which saved the lives of his comrades. Colonel Hatch approved the Certificates of Merit as did all the officers up the line until the line, to Washington, where the matter came to a halt. Army regulations blocked the awards requested for two reasons. First, Certificates of Merit are only issued to privates. Greaves was a corporal and therefore a non-commission officer.

Second, the regulations required that Certificates of Merit be issued only for individual recommendations rather than group awards. General William T. Sherman approved the Medal of Honor for Greaves and rejected the rest of Lieutenant Wright's recommendations.

Clinton Greaves received the Medal of Honor on June 26, 1879. After he received the Medal of Honor, Greaves must have worn it regularly. By the spring of 1881, he had worn out the medal's ribbon and sent to Philadelphia for a new one.

After spending 15 years with the 9th Cavalry, Corporal Greaves transferred to Columbus Barracks, Ohio, where he trained new recruits. Corporal Greaves served for five years at the Columbus Barracks before he was discharged for good on January 5, 1893.

During most of his military career, Greaves was single, but sometime before his final discharge in 1893, he married Bertha Williams, whose first husband had deserted her. Bertha was also a Virginian and was 15 years younger than her new husband.

After leaving the service, Greaves settled in Columbus, Ohio, where he worked as a civilian in the Quartermaster's office.

Clinton Greaves died of heart disease in Columbus on August 18, 1906, and is buried in the Greenlawn Cemetery, Columbus, Ohio. Bertha Greaves outlived her husband by 30 years. She supported herself by doing housework. Bertha is buried next to Clifton in the Greenlawn Cemetery.

Sergeant Henry Johnson, USA

9th U.S. Cavalry

Henry Johnson was born on June 11, 1850, at Boydton, Mecklenburg County, Virginia. Johnson was a 21-year-old laborer when he enlisted in the Army in 1867. By 1879, he was a sergeant in Company D, 9th U.S. Cavalry.

Sergeant Henry Johnson was one of the 10 men to earn the Medal of Honor in an action against hostile Ute Indians at the battle of Milk River, Colorado, which lasted from September 29 to October 5, 1879. His citation reads: "Voluntarily left fortified shelter and under heavy fire at close range made the rounds of the pits to instruct the guards; fought his way to the creek and back to bring water to the wounded."

In the spring of 1878, Nathan C. Meeker was appointed Indian Agent to the Ute reservation at Milk River, Colorado. Meeker made strenuous efforts to educate the Utes and turn them into farmers. Meeker's efforts to force the Utes to adopt a totally foreign lifestyle caused a great deal of bitterness among the Indians. The bitterness boiled over on September 10, 1879, when Meeker demanded that the Utes begin plowing up their ponies' grazing land. A Ute medicine man named Johnson objected that the ponies would starve if their grazing land was plowed. Meeker responded that the Indians had too many ponies and should shoot some of them. This was simply too much for the Utes. One of the Utes beat Meeker and threw him out the front door. Meeker became hysterical and telegraphed military authorities that he and the agency were in danger.

In response to this appeal, Major Thomas T. Thornburg, 4th U.S. Infantry, left Fort Frederick Steele in Wyoming on September 21, 1879, with three companies of the 5th U.S. Cavalry, one of infantry and 25 wagons. Thornburg's command reached Milk River on September 25, and crossed the stream towards the agency. The Utes, believing that they were about to be attacked, confronted the troopers on the trail. Major Thornburg and Lieutenant Cherry rode forward to attempt to communicate with the Utes. The Utes refused to talk and at once opened a rapid and galling fire on the troopers.

Several men were killed and it was soon apparent that the exposed position of the troopers was untenable. Thornburg ordered his men to retreat slowly and affect a union with D Company that was guarding the wagons. The men retired in excellent order. The Utes, having been frustrated in their plan to destroy the forward part of the command, moved around the left flank and concentrated on a knoll commanding the line of retreat, for the purpose of cutting off the troopers from the wagon train. Captain J. Scott Payne led a small group of volunteers, charged the knoll, dispersed the Indians, and then retired to the wagons. Major Thornburg started for the train just as Captain Payne made the charge, but was shot and instantly killed just after he crossed the creek, about 500 yards from the wagons. Captain Payne, the senior officer, now took command.

Lieutenant Cherry called for volunteers to cover the retreat to the wagon train. Sergeant Edward P. Grimes, Corporal Edward F. Murphy and Blacksmith Wilhelm O. Philipsen of D Company were the first to jump off their horses and, followed by some other men, formed a skirmish line which covered the retreat of their comrades. As Lieutenant

Cherry and the skirmishers slowly fell back to the wagon train, they began to run out of ammunition. Lieutenant Cherry called for a volunteer to go back to the wagons and bring back some ammunition. Sergeant Grimes left the skirmishers and went back to the wagon train for ammunition. The Utes concentrated their fire upon the courageous sergeant who, under heavy fire at point blank range, brought back a supply of ammunition. By this time, Lieutenant Cherry and his men were nearly cut off. The detachment was exposed to heavy fire and three of the troopers had been killed before they made it back to the makeshift fort.

The troopers guarding the wagons had also been busy. Under heavy attack, the soldiers unloaded the bedding boxes and sacks of grain and flour from the wagons and formed a breastwork. Most of the horses were killed and their carcasses were added to the makeshift fort. The Utes poured an intensive fire on the troopers, who were erecting the breastworks; Corporal Hampton M. Roach's coolness under fire in erecting the breastworks was exceptional. Once the makeshift fort was complete, Sergeant Lawton and Lieutenant Cherry, with their men who had been doing their best to keep the Utes at a distance, entered the corral, bringing all their wounded with them. Now united inside the little fort, the remainder of Thornburg's command fought off the swarming Utes. The heavy fighting continued until nightfall. The troopers used the lull to dig trenches around the wagons and a pit in the center of the makeshift fort, which served as a hospital for the wounded.

Sergeant John A. Poppe and a detachment of 10 men were ordered by Captain Payne to dislodge a group of Indians, who had taken a position in some nearby ravines and along the river bank, which allowed them to cut off some of the troopers from the wagon train. Sergeant Poppe gallantly charged the Utes, driving them from the ravine, which allowed the soldiers who had been cut off to rejoin the command.

The Utes next took advantage of a high wind blowing toward the wagons and set fire to the grass and sagebrush. The fire rapidly approached the wagons and the troopers were required to leave the corral to fight the flames. As soon as the troopers left their cover, the Indians unleashed their most furious attack of the day. Several men were killed and a number were wounded, but with great courage the troopers were able to extinguish the flames and repulse the Indian attack.

While the troopers were fighting the flames, Sergeant Poppe was ordered by Captain Payne to take three or four men and set fire to the grass around the wagons. Poppe said he would do it himself and, in an instant, was outside of the makeshift fort setting a counter fire. Although exposed to an intense fire from the Indians, Poppe moved from place to place setting fire and did not return to the safety of the fort until his duty was thoroughly completed.

By the end of the first day, 11 soldiers had been killed and 23 had been wounded. Twenty-three Utes had also been killed. The battle settled into a siege. During the day, the Utes would keep up such a galling fire that any movement around the makeshift fort was suicidal. Lieutenant Cherry called for volunteers to break through the Indian lines and go for help. Corporal George Moquin and Corporal Edward F. Murphy both volunteered to make the dangerous journey. Despite great danger, both men made it through the Indian lines and managed to get word of their comrades' plight to the Cavalry.

The first night of the siege, Corporal Hamilton M. Roach made the dangerous trip to the creek and, under an intense close range fire from the Utes, obtained water for his comrades. Corporal Roach repeated this feat of valor the next two nights as well.

On the morning of October 2, 1879, Captain Francis S. Dodge, Lieutenant M.B. Hughes and 35 buffalo soldiers of Company D, 9th U.S. Cavalry, after a grueling trek in which they marched over 100 miles in 23 hours, reached the besieged defenders. Morale inside the makeshift fort soared. The word had gotten out! Help was on its way! The small force of buffalo soldiers, while reinforcing the embattle command, was not strong enough to lift the siege. Notwithstanding arrival of the reinforcements, the battle continued unabated throughout the next three days.

A part of the 9th Cavalry's D Troop were sent forward to provide a screen for the main entrenchment. The troopers dug rifle pits in a relatively exposed forward position, where they drew the Ute's fire. Troop Sergeant Henry Johnson of the 9th U.S. Cavalry, as sergeant of the guard, was responsible for these outposts. Leaving the relative safety of his rifle pit, and under heavy fire, Sergeant Johnson made rounds of the trenches to see that his men were all right, and directed their fire against the enemy. Johnson's coolness and bravery under fire steadied and inspired the buffalo soldiers, as well as the other besieged troopers.

The wounded in the command began to suffer greatly from the lack of water. The Milk River was nearby, but the Utes were always watching. Only at night could soldiers risk sneaking down to the bank to fill canteens for the thirsty command. Several times men volunteered to crawl down to the river and fill canteens, but were driven back by fire from the Indians. Going after water was a hazardous mission. Two white soldiers had been killed attempting to get water for their suffering comrades. On the evening of October 4th, Sergeant Johnson once more left the relative safety of his rifle pit. As the best riflemen in the command covered him, Johnson crawled down to the river. Ute sharpshooters concentrated their fire on him, but with bullets striking all around him, the courageous sergeant continued to fill several canteens. Once back inside the makeshift fort, Sergeant Johnson again exposed himself as he moved from one wounded comrade to another, white or black, distributing the water.

In the finest tradition of the U.S. Army, both the officers and noncommissioned officers ignored danger and wounds to hold their beleaguered command together and keep up the morale of the men. Sergeant John Merrill, though painfully wounded, refused to leave his place on the front line. With tremendous grit, Sergeant Merrill remained on duty and performed gallantly throughout the siege.

On October 5, the situation looked bleak for the troopers of Payne's command. There were now 44 wounded and another 14 had died, including the surgeon, Dr. Grimes, who died of his wounds. The stench from the dead carcasses was almost intolerable. With the first rays of light came the sound of an Army bugle sounding "officer's call." The call was quickly answered by the trumpeter of Payne's command. The 5th Cavalry, under Colonel Wesley Merritt had arrived. The small fort was rocked with cheers.

Merritt's cavalry wheeled about and deployed for action. The Utes greeted the new arrivals with a volley of rife fire. The cavalry returned the fire and a short but fierce battled ensued. The Utes, having had enough, disappeared into the mountains.

There was a total of 10 Medals of Honor awarded for the action at Milk Creek. Captain Dodge, sergeants Grimes, Johnson, Lawton, Merrill and Widmer, corporals Moquin, Murphy and Roach, and Blacksmith Philipsen were awarded the Medal of Honor for their gallantry at Milk River.

The battle ended too late for Agent Meeker. While Thornburg's command was enduring a siege, Meeker and nine other agency employees were killed by the Utes, and the agency buildings were burned down. Mrs. Meeker, her daughter and another woman were taken captive. General Sherman had collected about 1,500 soldiers around the reservation and was ready to punish the Indians, even if it meant the death of the captives. Secretary of the Interior Carl Schurz overruled General Sherman's plan, however, and together with the new Indian Agent Charles

Grave of Sergeant Henry Johnson, USA

Adams, by October 21, negotiated the release of the women without further bloodshed.

Twelve Utes were singled out for trial on charges of murdering Meeker and for "outrages" committed against the women. The Utes escaped punishment, however, as they were granted amnesty in the larger settlement, but the tribe was moved onto a reservation in southwestern Colorado and eastern Utah.

At the end of his enlistment, Sergeant Johnson left the 9th Cavalry. He was discharged in January 1883 at Fort Riley, Kansas, five and one half years after his enlistment had begun. The extra six months were added to his time of service as the result of a court-martial conviction in March 1881, which resulted in Johnson losing his stripes and spending six months in the stockade. Johnson was mustered out as a private.

Two months after his discharge, Johnson reenlisted in the 10th Cavalry at Fort Grant, Arizona. He spent five years with the 10th and then transferred back to the 9th Cavalry. Johnson again was promoted to sergeant, but was busted again in 1889 as the result of a fight with a bartender at Fort Robinson, who refused to serve him more beer. Johnson was serving as a private in K Troop when he applied for a Medal of Honor for his actions 11 years earlier. His application was supported by Major Dodge and Captain Hughes.

Johnson was awarded the Medal of Honor on September 22, 1890.

Johnson was mustered out of service for the last time in July 1898 after 31 years of service. While he had served his country well, he had not been a model soldier. He had been reduced to the ranks three times, spent time in the stockade and had been disabled for a period of time with an illness, which, while common among soldiers at the time, was not contracted in the line of duty.

After leaving the Army Johnson settled in Washington, D.C. Henry

Johnson died on January 21, 1904, at Washington, D.C. At the time of his death, he was a public charge being housed at the Washington Asylum. He was buried with full military honors at Arlington National Cemetery in Arlington, Virginia.

Sergeant George Jordan, USA

9th U.S. Cavalry

George Jordan was born about 1847 in Williamson County, Tennessee. On December 25, 1866, at the age of 19, Jordan enlisted in the all black 9th U.S. Cavalry. Jordan was one of the original members of the 9th Cavalry, which was first organized in 1866. By 1880, he was a sergeant in Company K.

On the evening of May 13, 1880, Sergeant George Jordan was commanding a detachment of 25 men of Company K, 9th U.S. Cavalry at Sanders Stage Station, New Mexico, when a lone rider rode in on a lathered horse. He reported that Victorio, whom the troopers had thought they had pushed into Arizona, had doubled back and was headed for the small settlement adjacent to Fort Tularosa. Sergeant Jordan's command of dismounted cavalry had marched all day and were exhausted. Jordan explained to his men the situation, and told them they could decide whether they could march the remaining distance to Tularosa that night. The exhausted troopers agreed to a forced march. Sergeant Jordan marched his command throughout the night and arrived at Fort Tularosa early on the morning of the 14th. Victorio had not yet arrived. Sergeant Jordan immediately set his men to work repairing the stockade. Once the work was complete, Jordan gathered the frightened citizens into the stockade and positioned his men to best defend themselves.

At dusk, a party of more than 100 Apache Indians attacked the little fort, but were met by a determined fire from the troopers, which drove them back. The Indians attacked again, but the fire from the fort was undiminished and the Indians were driven back again. Victorio was seeking easy victims and plunder, and was not interested in fighting determined, well-led men. He, therefore, turned his warriors south leaving Sergeant Jordan in control of the fort.

For his courage and cool determination in directing his men in repulsing the attack at Fort Tularosa, Sergeant Jordan was awarded the Medal of Honor.

On December 30, 1890, Sergeant Jordan, serving with Major Guy Henry's battalion of the 9th Cavalry regiment, participated in the rescue of the 7th Cavalry from the Sioux ambush on the Pine Ridge, South Dakota reservation.

Jordan retired from the Cavalry in 1897 and settled in Crawford, Nebraska. George Jordan died at the U.S. Soldier's Home in Washington, D.C., on October 24, 1904. He is buried in the Fort McPherson National Cemetery, Maxwell, Nebraska.

Sergeant William McBryar, USA

10th U.S. Cavalry

William McBryar was born February 14, 1861, in Elizabethtown, North Carolina. In 1887, he enlisted in the Company K, 10th U.S. Cavalry in New York City. By 1890, McBryar was a sergeant and was posted in Arizona. He earned the Medal of Honor in a fight against the Apaches on March 7, 1890, at Salt River, Arizona.

On Sunday March 2, 1890, five renegade Apaches ambushed and killed a Mormon freighter named Fred Herbert, nine miles west of Fort Thomas, Arizona. Lieutenant J.W. Watson of San Carlos, in command of a detachment of Indian scouts, Lieutenant Clark and a detachment of K Company, 10th U.S. Cavalry, and Sergeant James T. Daniels, in command of a detachment of L Company, 4th U.S. Cavalry, were assigned to the pursuit.

After a dogged pursuit of more than 250 miles, the renegades were overtaken at Salt River, about 30 miles north of Globe, Arizona. The site the Apaches had chosen to make their camp was particularly rugged and almost impenetrable. In this forbidding terrain, the renegades thought they were safe, but the Apaches had not counted on the relentless pursuit of the troopers. Under the direction of Sergeant Rowdy, Company A, Indian Scouts, who also earned the Medal of Honor in this action, the troopers just kept coming.

At 1:00 P.M., on March 7, 1890, the Apaches were, in fact, taken completely by surprise. After the first volley, the Apaches took to the rocks and commenced a determined defense. Although there were not many of the renegades, the troopers were at a great disadvantage because of the terrain. The Apaches had to be flushed out of the rocks or they would simply disappear into the wilderness. Sergeant Daniels, another who would wear the Medal of Honor for this day's work, led the attack on the rocks. Sergeant McBryar distinguished himself for his coolness and bravery while under fire during the battle. Sergeant McBryar's marksmanship was also crucial to the outcome of the fight. In the firelight, the troopers killed two of the renegades and wounded a third before the two remaining Apache surrendered. The troopers and scouts did not suffer any casualties in the battle.

Grave of Sergeant William McBryar, USA

McBryar's military service included the Indian Wars, the Spanish-American War and the Philippine Insurrection. McBryar finished his career as a 1st lieutenant.

After leaving the service in 1899, McBryar worked as a watchman at Arlington Cemetery, a truck driver and a penitentiary guard. William McBryar died in Philadelphia on March 8, 1941, at the age of 80. He is buried at Arlington National Cemetery, Arlington, Virginia.

Corporal Isaiah Mays, USA

24th U.S. Infantry

Isaiah Mays was born on February 15, 1858, at Carters Bridge, Virginia. Mays was a laborer before enlisting in the Army in 1881 at Columbus Barracks, Franklin County, Ohio. Mays was assigned to Company C, 24th U.S. Infantry.

Corporal Mays earned the Medal of Honor on February 18, 1890. On that date Corporal Mays was serving as part of an escort consisting of two non-commissioned officers and nine privates. The escort was for Major Joseph W. Wham, Paymaster, U.S. Army, who was transporting an army payroll of $38,345.10 between forts Grant and Thomas in Arizona. The detail's progress was stopped by a large boulder weighing several tons that had been rolled onto the roadway. Just as the troopers were about to try to move the boulder out of the way, a single shot was fired from the ledge of rocks about 50 feet above and behind the troopers. The shot was followed immediately by a volley from what Major Wham later estimated was 15 to 20 guns. The troopers had been ambushed by a band of robbers, intent on capturing the payroll.

In his report on the incident, Major Wham stated, "I am convinced that two members of the escort did little or no fighting and almost immediately left the field, which reduced the number actually engaged, excluding my driver to nine." Private Lewis Hamilton, Major Wham's driver, was the first man hit in the action. He was shot through the stomach and was of no further use in the battle. Major Wham and the remainder of the escort made their stand and fought in the most courageous and heroic manner. For about thirty minutes, a sharp fight ensued, but the troopers had been caught in the open and the robbers were above them and entrenched in the rocks. The troopers attempted valiantly to defend their charge, but eight of the escort were wounded and two of those soldiers were shot twice.

When the firing started, Corporal Mays was positioned near the escort wagon. When the shooting became heavy, he took cover under the wagon, where he continued returning the robbers' fire. Later he moved to the side of Major Wham near the money wagon and continued the fight from that position. As more and more of the troopers were disabled it became clear to Corporal Mays that it was necessary that someone go for help. Corporal Mays, as one of the few soldiers still uninjured, took this task upon himself and crawled and walked for two miles to the Cottonwood Ranch where he sought help for his comrades. The help, however, arrived too late.

At the site of the ambush, the soldiers were forced to withdraw and abandon the payroll to the robbers. The robbers broke into the wooden strong box and made off with the money. This led to a number of investigations. Marshall Mead, who conducted a thorough investigation, swore that "I am satisfied a braver or a better defense could not have been made under like circumstances, and to have remained longer would have proven a useless sacrifice of life without a vestige of hope to succeed."

Lieutenant Cartwright was assigned to investigate the matter on behalf of the Army. Cartwright gave the matter his full attention until the completion of the trial of the men accused of committing the robbery. In his final report, Lieutenant Cartwright swore "That the escort fought well and bravely is attested by the bullet marks on the robbery position as well as by those on the rock occupied by Major Wham and the soldiers."

Major Wham concluded his report on the matter by recalling that he had served in the Civil War regiment which had been commanded by a certain Colonel Ulysses S. Grant. That regiment had participated in 16 battles and was justly proud of its record, but Wham said, "I never witnessed better courage or better fighting than shown by these colored soldiers, on May 11, 1889." Major Wham recommended several of the men for Certificates of Merit and recommended Sergeant Brown and Corporal Isaiah Mays for the Medal of Honor. The recommendations were accepted and the certificates and medals were issued on February 19, 1890.

When his term of service expired in September 1891, Corporal Mays immediately reenlisted, but shortly thereafter, he began to doubt the wisdom of his choice. In February 1892, he sought a discharge on the grounds that his parents were in their 70s and needed his assistance in looking after them in their old age. His request was turned down by the Army as he had just reenlisted, had taken a short furlough and could not be discharged after honoring so little of his commitment.

A few days after his application for discharge was denied, Corporal Mays got into a heated argument with Captain Henry Wygant, his commanding officer. Wygant had supported his request for a discharge but upon its denial by the Army was taking a firm stand. "God damn it," Corporal Mays raged. "I will not be ordered about like a dog. By God I will get out of here and I will fix you." He them stormed out of Captain Wygant's office, slamming the door behind him as he left.

Court-martialed for his insubordination, Mays lost his stripes and was fined ten dollars a month for six months. In June, he was reassigned to Company D and transferred to Fort Bayard, New Mexico.

In the summer of 1893, Mays again sought a discharge based upon his need to take care of his aged parents. This time his request was granted and he was released from the remainder of his obligation. Mays did not, however, go back to Virginia. Mays took jobs as a laborer in Clifton, Arizona, in 1895 and 1896. He was living in Guthrie, Arizona, in 1910.

In 1922, Mays, with the assistance of Congressman Carl Hayden of Arizona, unsuccessfully applied for an invalid pension. Isaiah Mays died on May 2, 1925, at Phoenix, Arizona. He is buried in the Arizona State Hospital Cemetery in Phoenix, Arizona.

Private Adam Paine, USA

Indian Scouts

Adam Paine was born in Florida in 1843. A Negro by race, Paine's ancestors had fled slavery and found refuge among the Seminole Indians of Florida. The Seminoles had accepted them as equals and given them a place to live. The blacks adopted the Seminole culture and were, for all intents and purposes, black Indians. When the Seminoles were driven out of Florida to Oklahoma and Texas, the black Seminoles went with them. As a child, Paine had traveled the Trail of Tears, as the expulsion and forced migration of the Indian tribes of the southeast became known.

Adam Paine was in his thirties when he enlisted in the Indian Scouts on November 12, 1873, at Fort Duncan, Texas. At the time of his enlistment he stood 5 feet 7 inches tall.

Private Adam Paine earned the Medal of Honor on September 20, 1874, during the Red River War of 1874–1875. White hunters virtually eliminated the buffalo herds from the southern plains and the U.S. government failed to provide the impoverished Indians with the rations it had promised to those who settled on the reservations. The Comanches left the reservation and went on the warpath, raiding and killing white settlers all along the frontier. The Comanches were able to convince many of the Kiowa, Cheyenne, and Arapaho to join them in their rebellion.

Colonel Mackenzie and the 4th U.S. Cavalry played a major role in defeating the Indians and forcing them back onto the reservations. On September 20, 1874, Mackenzie's main column left camp on Catfish Creek and headed north past the headwaters of the Witchita River, through the valley of Quitaque Creek and up the bluffs to the Staked Plains. The Staked Plains are a barren treeless table land that straddles the Texas–New Mexico boarder. In 1874, the Staked Plains was a wilderness which defied all comers.

Adam Paine and four scouts rode about a day's march ahead of Mackenzie's column. The colorful Paine, who was known by some of his fellow scouts as Bad Man, was wearing a buffalo horn headdress. On September 26th, the scouts were discovered by about 25 Comanche Indians and were attacked. Badly outnumbered, the scouts were forced to fight for their lives. Private Paine was fearless. On the first Indian charge, Paine calmly swung out of his saddle and, taking aim, fired his rifle, killing the horse of a charging Comanche. The Comanche warriors were determined to kill these intruders into the reservation and the fighting became intense. At one point, Paine took on six the Indians at one time, before the scouts were able to break out of the encirclement and make good their escape. Private Paine was able to lead the party safely back to camp.

Colonel Mackenzie, the commanding officer of the 4th Cavalry, was very impressed with Paine and recommended him for a Medal of Honor. On this occasion, Mackenzie wrote of Paine, "This man is a scout of great courage." On another occasion he wrote, "This man has, I believe, more cool daring than any scout I have ever known."

Private Paine earned the Medal of Honor September 26–27, 1874, at Canyon Blanco, Texas. His simple citation reads as follows: "Rendered invaluable service to Colonel Ranald S. Mackenzie, 4th U. S. Cavalry, during this engagement."

After serving two enlistments with the Indian scouts, Paine was discharged on February 19, 1875. After leaving the service, Paine allegedly killed a black soldier in Brownsville with a knife and became a fugitive from justice. During the early morning hours of January 1, 1877, Paine was shot in the back and killed by Clarion Windus, a local deputy sheriff while he was attending a New Year's Eve dance at the Seminole Indian Camp at Brackettville, Texas. The sheriff, rather than trying to take Paine alive, shot Paine in the back with a double-barreled shot gun at such close range that his clothes were set on fire.

Killed on January 1, 1877, Adam Paine, the second black soldier to earn the Medal of Honor during the Indian Wars, was buried in the Seminole Indian Scout Cemetery, Brackettville, Texas.

Trumpeter Isaac Payne, USA

Indian Scouts

Isaac Payne was born in Mexico in 1854. At the age of 17, Payne enlisted in the Seminole Indian Scouts at Fort Duncan, Texas.

Trumpeter Payne earned the Medal of Honor on April 25, 1875, at the Pecos River, Texas. His citation reads as follows: "With three other men, he participated in a charge against 25 hostiles while on a scouting patrol."

In a battle on the Pecos River in Texas on April 25, 1875, Trumpeter Isaac Payne, Sergeant John Ward, and Private Pompey Factor were cited for "gallantry in action" against Indians. Lieutenant Bullis and the three scouts left Fort Clark on April 16 on a scouting mission. On the 25th, the scouts came across the trail they had been seeking. It was a large trail, which Lieutenant Bullis estimated to have been made by 75 horses or more. The scouts followed the trail and soon came upon the party of Indians who were in the process of crossing the Pecos River. The scouts quickly found favorable ground and opened the fight. For about three quarters of an hour, the scouts were able to hold their own against the superior numbers, during which time they killed three of the Indians and wounded a fourth.

The four soldiers bravely held their ground, but were outnumbered and outgunned. They were finally forced to withdraw when they noticed a group of Indians moving to cut them off from their horses. Lieutenant Bullis, Sergeant Ward, Private Factor and Trumpeter Payne retreated to where they had tied their horses; the scouts mounted and were on their way out of the trap. Lieutenant Bullis, however, lost his horse in the confusion. The Lieutenant was able to attract Sergeant Ward's attention. Sergeant Ward turned his horse around and Lieutenant Bullis was able to mount behind him and they made good their escape.

Lieutenant Bullis described Sergeant Ward, Trumpeter Payne and Private Factor as "brave and trustworthy" and stated that each was worthy of a medal.

Isaac Payne was in the field with a detachment from Fort Clark when his enlistment expired in July of 1875. Three days after his term of enlistment had ended, Payne went home without permission. He later found out that the Army had charged him with desertion. When he attempted to reenlist, the Army had to put him back on the roles as having returned from desertion and discharged him as of the date his original term of enlistment had expired.

Except for brief periods between enlistments, Payne remained in the service until his final discharge on January 21, 1901. After leaving the service, Payne lived with his family at the Seminole-Negro Indian Camp. In 1903, Payne applied for an invalid's pension, claiming that he had been completely incapacitated by rheumatism stemming from his service as a scout and was unable to work.

Isaac Payne died on January 12, 1904, at Bacunuebtim, Nacimiento, Caohuila, Mexico. He is buried in the Seminole Indian Scout Cemetery, Brackettville, Texas.

Sergeant Thomas Shaw, USA

9th U.S. Cavalry

Thomas was born a slave in Covington, Kentucky, about 1846. A certain Mary J. Shaw, who even after President Lincoln's Emancipation Proclamation of 1862, continued to hold the erroneous belief that she could own another human being, applied for compensation from the U.S. government when her 18-year-old slave ran off and enlisted in the Union Army in 1864. The request for compensation was not granted. Thomas, who enlisted as Thomas Shaw, stayed in the Army after the Civil War, ending up on the western frontier in Company K, 9th U.S. Cavalry.

Captain Charles Parker and 19 men from Company K, 9th Cavalry, caught up with Nana and his renegade Apaches on August 12, 1881, near Carrizo Canyon in the Cuchillo Negra mountains. Riding with Company K were Sergeant George Jordan, who had earned the Medal of Honor in the defense of Tularosa, and Sergeant Thomas Shaw. Sergeant Shaw was the senior non-commissioned officer and rode next to Captain Parker, while Sergeant Jordan had command of the right flank.

The troopers chased the Apaches into Carrizo Canyon where they dismounted among the rocks and brush of the canyon, determined to make their stand. Captain Parker ordered his men to dismount and open fire. Although outnumbered by the Apaches by a ratio of about three to one, Captain Parker ordered his cavalrymen to press the attack against the Indians. A battle lasting one and a half hours ensued. Several times, the troopers managed to thwart the Indians as they attempted to turn the troopers' flank.

Two of the troopers—Charles Perry and Guy Temple—were killed early in the battle and another three cavalrymen were wounded. The Apaches, seeing their success and perceiving that they greatly outnumbered the troopers, moved to surround the small command. Sergeants Thomas Shaw and George Jordan were instrumental in thwarting this effort. A good shot, Sergeant Shaw selected for himself a position from which he had a

relatively clear field of fire upon the Apaches. The only problem with this choice was that the Apaches all had a clear shot at Sergeant Shaw as well. From this extremely exposed position, Shaw kept up a hot and accurate fire, which drove the Apaches back and kept them from surrounding the command.

Again, once Nana was certain that he could not gain any additional advantages in this action, and that the soldiers, because of their dead and wounded, could not follow him, he broke off the attack. Nana and his followers again disappeared into the desert.

Sergeant Shaw earned the Medal of Honor for his fearless defense of his comrades. Sergeant Jordan, who already held the Medal of Honor, was awarded a Certificate of Merit with its $2 per month pay increase. Both awards were issued December 7, 1890. Thomas Shaw's Medal of Honor citation reads as follows: "Forced the enemy back after stubbornly holding his ground in an extremely exposed position and prevented the enemy's superior numbers from surrounding his command."

Grave of Sergeant Thomas Shaw, USA

Thomas Shaw retired from the Army in 1894, after more than 28 years of service. Shaw settled down in Rosslyn, Virginia, where he died on June 23, 1895. Sergeant Thomas Shaw is buried at Arlington National Cemetery, Arlington, Virginia.

Sergeant Emanuel Stance, USA

9th U.S. Cavalry

Emanuel Stance was born in Charleston, South Carolina, about 1847. Stance had been a farmer in Louisiana when, on October 2, 1866, at the age of 19, he enlisted in Company F, 9th U.S. Cavalry.

On May 20, 1870, Captain Carroll dispatched two detachments from Fort McKavett north towards Kickapoo Springs in a desperate attempt to cut off a group of Apaches, who had kidnapped eight-year-old Willie Lehmann and his ten-year-old brother, Herman, from their stepfather's ranch in Loyal Valley. Sergeant Emanuel Stance, in command of a detachment of nine buffalo soldiers of Company F, 9th U.S. Cavalry, departed Fort McKavett, Texas, on a desperate mission to rescue the Lehmann children. Not far from the fort they ran into a band of Indians driving a small herd of horses up a hill. The troopers immediately pursued; after a brief running fight, the outnumbered Indians abandoned their horses and disappeared into the mountains.

After rounding up the horses, Sergeant Stance camped his command for the night near Kickapoo Springs. Burdened by their captive horses, the troopers were up and heading back for the fort early the next morning. The cavalrymen ran into a band of 20 Indians who were attempting to run off a herd of government horses. The few troopers guarding the horses had their hands full, attempting to fend off the Indian attack and keep the herd together at the same time.

Sergeant Stance instantly sized up the situation and ordered, "Charge!" The Indians tried to make a stand, as Stance stated in his report: "I set the Spencers talking and whistling about their ears so lively that they broke in confusion and fled to the hills leaving me with their herd of five horses."

The Indians, however, regrouped and appeared on the troopers' left flank, intent on recapturing their horses. The Indians opened fire at long range. The skirmishing continued until the troopers reached a water hole called Eight Mile. At this point, Sergeant Stance had more than enough of these Indians. He wheeled his command around and again gave the command, "Charge!" Sergeant Emanuel Stance, immediately upon giving the order, was off after the Indians, leading by his example. Charge means to go for it! No holding back. Sergeant Stance led the charge on left flank. Racing well ahead of the others, shooting and yelling encouragement to his men, Sergeant Stance took the attack home to the Indians. Unable to withstand an attack by the determined buffalo soldiers, the Indians quickly withdrew.

Again Stance's report of the incident was very modest, stating, "I turned my little command loose on them in this place, and after a few volleys they left me to continue my march in peace."

When Sergeant Stance and his troopers returned to Fort McKavett, they did not know that they had, in fact, accomplished a part of their mission. On the morning of May 21, Willie Lehman walked into the stage station at Kickapoo Springs. The tired, cold, hungry and bruised boy explained that the day before, a group of buffalo soldiers had charged the Indians who had taken him captive. When the warrior whose horse he was sharing began to lag behind, he pushed young Willie off his horse in order to make his escape. (Other accounts mention that both children returned.)

Captain Carroll was impressed with Sergeant Stance's courage and leadership which he displayed during the patrol of May 20 and 21st. In recommending Emanual Stance for the Medal of Honor, he wrote, "The gallantry displayed by the sergeant and his party as well as good judgment used on both occasions, deserves much praise."

Sergeant Stance's decisive and bold behavior in the face of an armed enemy represents the finest tradition of the American soldier. He was awarded the Medal of Honor on June 20, 1870, for his valor in leading the charge — the first African American to receive the Medal for valor in the Indian Wars.

Stance was deeply moved by the award. He expressed his feeling in a letter wherein he stated, "I will cherish the gift as a thing of priceless value and endeavor by my future conduct to merit the high honor conferred upon me."

The Medal of Honor did not turn Stance into a model soldier, however. The sergeant could have a violent temper. In December 1872, Sergeant Stance had a nasty brawl with Sergeant Henry Green. Green had reported him drunk on duty at the stables and Stance was furious. Stance insisted that Sergeant Green had lied and soon the two men came to blows. In the fight, Stance bit off a part of Sergeant Green's lower lip. This was only one of several fights that Stance was involved in. His military records show that he was reduced in rank five times, but each time regained his former rank.

Sergeant Emanuel Stance was murdered by "unknown party or parties" on December 25, 1887, near Fort Robinson, Nebraska. He had been shot with a service revolver. It was assumed by all that he had been killed by the men of his own company. Sergeant Stance was a strict disciplinarian and his style of command had angered many of his men. Private Miller Milds of F Troop was charged with the murder, but was released for the lack of witnesses. Emanuel Stance is buried at Fort McPherson National Cemetery, Maxwell, Nebraska.

Private Augustus Walley, USA

9th U.S. Cavalry

Augustus Walley was born into slavery on March 10, 1856, at Reistertown, Baltimore County, Maryland. He entered the Army at Baltimore, Maryland, and was assigned to Company I, 9th U.S. Cavalry.

Private Walley earned the Medal of Honor on August 16, 1881, at Cuchillo Negro Mountains, New Mexico. His simple citation reads, "Bravery in action with Apaches."

At about noon August 16, 1881, a Mexican came into the camp of Company I, 9th U.S. Cavalry, yelling that a band of Apaches under Nana had attacked the Chavez Ranch just two miles away from where Company I was camped. The Apaches had killed Mr. Chavez, his wife, his two children and two of the ranch hands. Company I, which was under the command of Lieutenant Gustavus Valois, had been resting after a strenuous campaign searching for Nana and his band of Apaches. Lieutenant Valois ordered 2nd Lieutenant Burnett to take 12 men and ride immediately to the ranch. He was to pick up the perpetrators' trail and pursue them. Lieutenant Valois would follow with the rest of the company just as fast as he could.

At the ranch, Lieutenant Burnett confirmed the massacre. It appeared that between 40 to 60 Indians had attacked the ranch. The settlers never had a chance. The Apaches had lived up to their usual brutal standards, torturing to death women and children in the most cruel manner imaginable. While at the ranch, Burnett's force was joined by a group of angry Mexican-Americans who were mounted, armed and determined to take revenge on the Indians. The whole group, now numbering about 50 men, set out in pursuit. The Indian trail was quickly picked up. The Apaches were headed for the Cuchillo Negro Mountains with their plunder.

Lieutenant Burnett and his command quickly caught up with the Apaches who were encumbered by their plunder. At the appearance of the soldiers, the Apaches dismounted, determined to stand their ground along a ridge-line. Burnett split his command into three groups. The Hispanics were on the left and Sergeant Moses Williams on the right. Lieutenant Burnett personally commanded the center. The whole group went galloping after the now stationary Indians. At 1000 yards, the Apaches opened fire, forcing the soldiers to dismount and advance on foot. Lieutenant Burnett sent Sergeant Williams to the right to flank the Indians on that side, and sent the Mexican-Americans around the other flank, while he and his men kept up a continuous fire from the center. When Sergeant Williams was in position to flank the line, he gave Lieutenant Burnett the signal and Lieutenant Burnett and his men charged forward at the same time Sergeant Williams attacked from the flank. Under the pressure, the Apaches broke and retreated to the next ridgeline.

The process was repeated again and again and soon a running battle, which lasted for several hours, was in progress. Each time the Apaches would take up a position on a ridge, Sergeant Williams would flank them while Lieutenant Burnett attacked from the front. In this manner, the troopers pushed the Apaches back from ridge to ridge for eight to ten miles. When the Apaches reached the foothills of the Cuchillo Negro at about 4:00 P.M., they made their final stand. They were determined to hold this position at all costs. The position they had chosen for the stand was a strong one and Lieutenant Burnett found that the position was too strong for his force to take. Lieutenant Valois and the rest of the company had not yet come up. Lieutenant Burnett determined to keep the Apaches pinned down, while a courier was sent to find Lieutenant Valois and guide him to a hill to the right of the Apaches' position. This hill when occupied would make their position untenable.

In the meantime, Lieutenant Burnett attempted to take a part of his command to get behind the Indians to prevent them from retreating farther into the mountains, where they would be lost. The troopers thought they had gotten behind the Apaches without being spotted, when Sergeant Williams pointed out what appeared to be an Indian's head peering at the troopers from the rocks. Lieutenant Burnett immediately jumped off his horse and, using his saddle as a gun rest, shot and killed the Indian. The shot, however, brought a volley in response as Indians fired at the troopers from all along the ridge. Nana had set a trap for the troopers and only Sergeant Williams' keen eyes had kept them from walking into it.

Burnett ordered his men to dismount and take cover among rocks. But before the order could be obeyed, the lieutenant's horse broke loose and ran away. Someone yelled, "They got the lieutenant! They got the lieutenant!" The entire command, except Sergeant Williams and Private Walley, began to retreat down the canyon. Burnett sent Sergeant Williams down the canyon to bring back his men and he and Private Walley took cover behind a rock and returned the Indians' fire. When

Sergeant Williams returned with the rest of the command, the Indians were dislodged from their position on the ridge.

The Indians fled to the left and Lieutenant Burnett's first impulse was to follow them, but the sounds of battle made it clear that Valois had arrived and was having a tough time of it. Lieutenant Burnett led his command towards the sound of battle and arrived none too soon. Nana had anticipated Valois' attempt to flank his Apaches and had occupied a hill just as Valois' men were racing to the top. The soldiers were met with a volley that killed almost all of the horses and wounded several of the troopers. When Burnett arrived, Valois' men were being pressed from all sides and were retreating before the Indian onslaught. Burnett had his men charge, which drove the Indians back. He than dismounted his men and held a line, pinning down the Indians. Lieutenant Burnett's timely action allowed Valois to gather his wounded and get them to the rear.

Lieutenant Valois ordered a withdrawal and sent word for Lieutenant Burnett to follow suit. Burnett ordered his detachment to retreat to a ridge behind them. Lieutenant Burnett, Sergeant Williams and Private Walley held the Indians at bay while the remainder of the detachment withdrew. Just as these men forming the rear guard were ready to pull back, a voice was heard calling, "Lieutenant ... please for God's sake don't leave us! Our lives depend on you."

"Who's there," the lieutenant called back.

"Privates Burton, Glasby and Wilson, Sir," was the reply.

To his surprise and dismay Burnett found that three of Valois' men had been left behind. They were pinned down behind some prairie dog mounds about 200 yards away and could not retreat without exposing themselves to hostile fire. Lieutenant Burnett, not willing to allow any of his men to be captured, called for volunteers to rescue the stranded men; Sergeant Williams and Private Augustus Walley answered the call.

Burnett and his volunteers took up positions so that they could cover the stranded troopers. Burnett then ordered them to crawl to safety. Seeing their prey about to get away, the Apaches began to advance on their position, but the covering fire from Burnett's small group forced them to keep their distance. Glasby and Wilson made it back to the troopers' lines.

Private Burton was wounded and unable to withdraw. Private Walley, after receiving permission to attempt the rescue, mounted his horse and rode low in the saddle, defying a hail of bullets from the Indians. He charged to the position of Private Burton, assisted him into the saddle and mounting behind him rode to safety at the rear. The lieutenant and the sergeant kept up an intense covering fire to aid Private Walley's valiant rescue attempt.

Lieutenant Burnett located a fourth trooper in a state of shock, wandering aimlessly about the field in the general direction of the Indian lines. This was Private Martin of Valois' command who had also lost his horse and was caught behind enemy lines. With Sergeant Williams covering him, Lieutenant Burnett mounted and road out to the trooper, placing himself and his horse between the dazed man and the Indians. Burnett was able to get the trooper turned around and the two of them made it to the safety of the rear.

Lieutenant Valois found a defensible position and the troopers made a stand. Nana, seeing that he had done all the damage he could do, and sensing that Valois could no longer follow him, broke off the engagement and disappeared into the mountains.

For their actions in saving the lives of their comrades at the risk of their own lives, Lieutenant Burnett, Sergeant Williams and Private Walley were awarded the Medal of Honor. Lieutenant Burnett in his letter of recommendation for Private Walley, who later became a farrier, stated:

> I might cite many minor instances of Farrier Walley's gallantry and bravery on this and other campaigns for he was always to the front, ready, willing and anxious to do his full duty — and even more — but I will content myself with the above, adding that during a period of nearly two (2) years while under my immediate command — whether in the garrison or field — I always found Farrier Walley a thoroughly reliable, trustworthy and efficient soldier and during his services with me — on and off—for eight years I never knew him to receive even as much as a rebuke, and I have always heard him spoken of in terms of praise by my brother officers, and I venture the assertion that no young soldier is better known in the regiment.

Private Walley's Medal of Honor was issued on October 1, 1890.

Walley remained in the Army until his retirement in 1907, after 30 years of service. His first 15 years were spent in Company I, 9th U.S. Cavalry, and the last 15 years in Company I, 10th U.S. Cavalry. While serving with the 10th Cavalry in Cuba, Walley participated in Teddy Roosevelt's charge up San Juan Hill. He was also recommended for a second Medal of Honor for assisting Captain Charles G. Ayers in carrying a wounded major from the 1st Cavalry off the field under a terrific enemy fire. The second medal was not approved. Walley also served in the Philippines. He was stationed in Fort Washakie, Wyoming, at the time of his retirement.

After his retirement, Walley lived in Butte, Montana; Prague, Oklahoma; Cleveland, Ohio and Baltimore, Maryland.

Walley was recalled to active duty during World War I. He served as a sergeant at Camp Beauregard, Louisiana, from May 1, 1918, to March 7, 1919.

Augustus Walley died on April 9, 1938, at Baltimore, Maryland. He is buried at St. Luke's Cemetery, Reisterstown, Maryland.

Sergeant John Ward, USA

Indian Scouts

John Warrior was born in 1847 in Arkansas. A farmer before entering the Army, John Warrior first enlisted in the Indian Scouts on August 16, 1870, at Fort Duncan, Texas. A recruiting officer shortened his name to John Ward and he went by that name for the rest of his military career. Ward's scouts were assigned to serve with the 24th Infantry.

Sergeant John Ward earned the Medal of Honor on April 25, 1875, at the Pecos River, Texas. His simple citation reads as follows: "With three others he participated in a charge against 25 hostiles while on a scouting patrol."

Lieutenant Bullis and three scouts had set out from Fort Duncan on April 16, 1875, to locate a band of Indians who had been raiding the settlers and had stolen 75 horses. On the 25th, the scouts came across the trail they had been seeking. They followed the trail and soon came upon the party of Indians who were in the process of crossing the Pecos River. A battle ensued and for about three quarters of an hour the four soldiers bravely held their ground, but were outnumbered and outgunned. Lieutenant Bullis, Sergeant Ward, Private Factor and Trumpeter Payne retreated to where they had tied their horses; the scouts mounted their horses and were on their way out of the trap. Lieutenant Bullis, however, lost his horse in the confusion. Sergeant Ward turned his horse around and Lieutenant Bullis was able to mount behind him and they made good their escape.

Lieutenant Bullis described Sergeant John Ward, Trumpeter Isaac

Payne and Private Pompey Factor as "brave and trustworthy" and stated that each was worthy of a medal.

Except for brief intervals between enlistments required by the Army for Indian Scouts, Sergeant Ward served continuously until his final discharge on October 5, 1894. John Ward worked as a gardener in Brackettsville after his discharge. He died on May 24, 1911, at Seminole-Negro Indian camp. Ward is buried in the Seminole Indian Scout Cemetery located in Brackettville, Texas.

1st Sergeant Moses Williams, USA

9th U.S. Cavalry

Moses Williams was born in 1849 at Carrollton, Orleans Parish, Louisiana. He entered the Army at East Carroll Parish, Louisiana, and was assigned to Company I, 9th U.S. Cavalry.

Sergeant Williams earned the Medal of Honor on August 16, 1881, at Cuchillo Negro Mountains, New Mexico. His simple citation reads as follows: "Rallied a detachment, skillfully conducted a running fight of three or four hours, and by his coolness, bravery and unflinching devotion to duty in standing by his commanding officer in an exposed position under heavy fire from a large party of Indians saved the lives of at least three of his comrades."

At about noon August 16, 1881, a Mexican came into the camp of Company I, of the 9th U.S. Cavalry, yelling that a band of Apaches under Nana had attacked the Chavez Ranch just two miles away from where Company I was camped. The Apaches had killed Mr. Chavez, his wife, his two children and two of the ranch hands. Company I, which was under the command of Lieutenant Gustavus Valois, had been resting after a strenuous campaign searching for Nana and his band of Apaches. Lieutenant Valois ordered 2nd Lieutenant George R. Burnett to take 12 men and ride immediately to the ranch. He was to pick up the perpetrators' trail and pursue them. Lieutenant Valois would follow with the rest of the company.

At the ranch Lieutenant Burnett confirmed the massacre. It appeared that between 40 to 60 Indians had attacked the ranch. The settlers never had a chance. The Apaches had tortured to death women and children in the most cruel manner imaginable. While at the ranch, Burnett's force was joined by a group of angry Mexican-Americans who were mounted, armed and determined to take revenge on the Indians. The whole group, now numbering about fifty men, set out in pursuit. The Indian trail was quickly picked up. The Apaches were headed for the Cuchillo Negro Mountains with their plunder.

Lieutenant Burnett and his command quickly caught up with the Apaches, who were moving slowly, being encumbered with their plunder. At the appearance of the soldiers, the Apaches dismounted, determined to stand their ground along a ridge line. Burnett split his command into three groups with the Hispanics on the left and Sergeant Moses Williams on the right, while he personally commanded the center. The whole group went galloping after the now stationary Indians. At 1000 yards the Apaches opened fire, forcing the soldiers to dismount and advance on foot. Lieutenant Burnett sent Sergeant Williams to the right to flank the Indians on that side and sent the Mexican-Americans around the left flank, while he and his men kept up a continuous fire from the center. When Sergeant Williams was in position to flank the line, he gave Lieutenant Burnett the signal and Lieutenant Burnett and his men would charge forward at the same time Sergeant Williams would attack from the flank. Under the pressure, the Apaches broke and retreated to the next ridge line.

The process was repeated again and again and soon a running battle, which lasted for several hours, was in progress. Each time the Apaches would take up a position on a ridge, Sergeant Williams would flank them, while Lieutenant Burnett attacked from the front. In this manner the troopers pushed the Apaches back from ridge to ridge for eight to ten miles. When the Apaches reached the foothills of the Cuchillo Negro Mountains at about 4:00 P.M., they made their final stand. They were determined to hold this position at all costs. The position the Apaches had chosen was a strong one and Lieutenant Burnett found that he could not dislodge the Indians with a direct assault. For some reason, Lieutenant Valois and the rest of the Company had not yet come up. Lieutenant Burnett determined to keep the Apaches pinned down while a courier was sent to find Lieutenant Valois and guide him to a hill to the right of the Apaches' position. If Valois could occupy that hill, the Indians' position would be untenable.

In the meantime, leaving the Mexican-Americans to hold the Apaches' front, Lieutenant Burnett attempted to take his small command to get into the Indians' rear so that they could not retreat into the mountains and be lost. On approaching the Indians' rear, Sergeant

Williams pointed out what appeared to be an Indian's head peering at the troopers from the rocks. Lieutenant Burnett immediately jumped off his horse and using his saddle as a gun rest, shot and killed the Indian. The shot, however, brought a volley in response as Indians fired at the troopers from all along the ridge. Nana had set a trap for the troopers and only Sergeant Williams' keen eyes had kept them from walking into it.

Lieutenant Burnett ordered his men to dismount and take cover among rocks. But before the order could be obeyed, the lieutenant's horse broke loose and ran away. Someone yelled, "They got the lieutenant! They got the lieutenant!" The entire command, except Sergeant Williams and Private Walley, began to retreat down the canyon. Burnett sent Sergeant Williams down the canyon to bring back his men while he and Private Walley took cover behind a rock and returned the Indians' fire. When Sergeant Williams returned with the rest of the command their combined fire appeared to dislodge the Indians from their position on the ridge.

The Indians fled to the left and Lieutenant Burnett's first impulse was to follow them, but the sounds of battle made it clear that Valois had arrived and was having a tough time of it. Lieutenant Burnett led his command towards the sound of battle and arrived none too soon. The crafty old Nana had anticipated Valois' attempt to flank his Apaches and had occupied a hill just as Valois' men were racing to the top. The soldiers were met with a volley that killed almost all of the horses and wounded several of the troopers. When Burnett arrived, Valois' men were being pressed from all sides and were retreating before the Indian onslaught. Burnett had his men charge, which drove the Indians back. He then dismounted his men and held a line, pinning down the Indians. Lieutenant Burnett's timely action allowed Lieutenant Valois to gather his wounded and get them to the rear.

Lieutenant Valois ordered a withdrawal and sent word for Lieutenant Burnett to follow suit. Burnett ordered his detachment to retreat to a ridge behind them. Lieutenant Burnett, Sergeant Williams and Private Walley held the Indians at bay while the remainder of the detachment withdrew. Just as these men forming the rear guard were ready to pull back, a voice was heard calling, "Lieutenant ... please for God's sake don't leave us! Our lives depend on you."

"Who's there?" the lieutenant called back.

"Privates Burton, Glasby and Wilson, Sir," was the reply.

To his surprise and dismay, Burnett found that three of Valois' men had been left behind. They were pinned down behind some prairie dog mounds about 200 yards away and could not retreat without exposing themselves to hostile fire. Lieutenant Burnett, not willing to allow any of his men to be captured, called for volunteers to rescue the stranded men. Sergeant Williams and Private Augustus Walley answered the call.

Burnett and his volunteers took up positions so that they could cover the stranded troopers. Burnett then ordered them to crawl to safety. Seeing their prey about to get away, the Apaches began to advance on their position, but the covering fire from Burnett's small group forced them to keep their distance. Glasby and Wilson made it back to the troopers' lines.

Private Burton was wounded and unable to withdraw. Private Walley, after receiving permission to attempt the rescue, mounted his horse and rode low in the saddle, defying a hail of bullets from the Indians. Private Walley charged to the position of Private Burton, assisted him into the saddle, and, mounting behind him, rode to safety at the rear. The lieutenant and the sergeant kept up an intense covering fire to aid Private Walley's valiant rescue attempt.

Lieutenant Burnett located a fourth trooper in a state of shock, wandering aimlessly about the field in the general direction of the Indian lines. This was Private Martin, also of Valois' command, who had also lost his horse and was caught behind enemy lines. With Sergeant Williams covering him, Lieutenant Burnett mounted and rode out to the trooper, placing himself and his horse between the dazed man and the Indians. Burnett was able to get the trooper turned around and the two of them made it to the safety of the rear.

Lieutenant Valois found a defensible position and the troopers made a stand. Nana, seeing that he had done all the damage he could do, and, sensing that Lieutenant Valois could no longer follow him, broke off the engagement and disappeared into the mountains.

For their actions in saving the lives of their comrades at the risk of their own lives, Lieutenant Burnett, Sergeant Williams and Private Walley were awarded the Medal of Honor. Moses Williams' medal was issued on November 12, 1896.

Moses Williams died on August 23, 1899, at Vancouver Barracks, Washington. He is buried at the Vancouver Barracks Cemetery in Vancouver, Washington. A special headstone showing that Williams earned the Medal of Honor marks his grave.

Corporal William O. Wilson, USA

9th U.S. Cavalry

William Othello Wilson was born at Hagerstown, Maryland, in September 1867. He enlisted in Company I, 9th U.S. Cavalry, at St Paul, Minnesota, on August 21, 1889, one month before his 22nd birthday.

In 1890, a new religion spread through the Indians of the Great Plains like wildfire through dry grass. The phenomenon, called the Ghost Dance religion, swept eastward from Nevada. This new religion promised that, through song and dance, the great buffalo herds would return and the civilization of the white men on this continent would be destroyed. The downtrodden Indians sang and danced themselves into a frenzy.

Cavalry and infantry units from all over the country were ordered to the Sioux reservations to quell the expected disturbances. Among them, the 9th Cavalry was ordered from Fort Robinson, Nebraska. By November 30, nearly half of the nation's cavalry and infantry units had converged upon the Sioux. Frightened Indians fled the reservations. The Cavalry was sent to bring them back.

On December 28, the 7th Cavalry located Big Foot and his band of Sioux. The next day, while the soldiers were disarming the Indians, the bloodbath known as the Battle of Wounded Knee took place. As word of the battle spread among the Indians, the 7th Cavalry skirmished with groups of enraged Sioux warriors from Wounded Knee to the Pine Ridge reservation. Orders were sent to Major Henry for the 9th Cavalry to immediately return to Pine Ridge agency. To make better time, Major Henry left his wagon train with Company I, under the command of Captain John S. Loud, and rushed ahead to the reservation.

On December 30, 1890, the day after the Battle of Wounded Knee, Colonel James W. Forsyth and eight companies of the 7th U.S. Cavalry were sent to the Drexel Mission to investigate columns of smoke that were rising from that vicinity. The command reached the mission and found that the Indians had set fire to a small building. The Indians retreated when the troopers arrived. Colonel Forsyth followed the Sioux down a narrow valley with steep bluffs to the east and west. Once Forsyth's command was well inside the valley, the Sioux sprang their trap and opened fire on the soldiers from their positions on the bluffs. Colonel Forsyth's efforts to break out were thwarted and his position was growing desperate.

The sound of gunfire alerted Major Guy Henry, a soldier's soldier, who already held the Medal of Honor. His command of buffalo soldiers of the 9th U.S. Cavalry, with no more than two hours' sleep, immediately set off in the direction of the battle. When Henry's command reached the mouth of the valley, he sent Captain Wright with I and K companies up the east ridges, and Captain C.S. Stedman with D and F companies up the bluffs to the west. The buffalo soldiers drove the Sioux back, relieving the pressure on their comrades of the 7th Cavalry.

No sooner had the Sioux been driven back than Corporal William O. Wilson rode in with word that the wagon train was under attack! Within minutes the buffalo soldiers were back in their saddles and off to rescue their comrades. They arrived in time to save Company I from annihilation.

Major Henry praised Corporal Wilson's courage in an order to be read to each of the companies of the 9th:

> On the morning of December 30, hostile Indians attacked the wagon train of this command. To obtain assistance, it was necessary to send word to the Agency. The duty to be performed was one enduring much risk as the Indians, knowing what was intended, would endeavor to intercept the messenger, and overwhelmed by numbers certain death would follow. Corporal W. O. Wilson, "I" 9th Cavalry, volunteered for the above duty, and though pursued by Indians, succeeded. Such examples of soldier-like conduct are worth of imitation and reflect credit not only on Corporal Wilson but the 9th Cavalry. This order will be read to each troop.

On September 17, 1891, Corporal William O. Wilson of Company I, 9th U.S. Cavalry, was awarded the Medal of Honor for his valor in going for help to save his comrades. His citation, however, simply reads, "Bravery."

Two years later Corporal Wilson was stationed at Fort Ducchesne, Utah, where he was smarting from disciplinary action in which he felt he had been unfairly treated. Wilson traveled to Denver, Colorado, to participate in an Army sponsored marksmanship event. On September 5, 1893, he deserted from the Army and disappeared from history.

Recently, Medal of Honor researcher Preston Amos found that Wilson returned to Hagerstown, Maryland, where he lived out the remainder of his life, keeping a low profile.

William Othello Wilson died in Hagerstown, Washington County, Maryland, on January 18, 1928. He is buried in the Jewish Cemetery at Halfway, Maryland.

Sergeant Brent Woods, USA

9th U.S. Cavalry

Brent Woods was born in Pulaski County, Kentucky, in 1850 to a slave family. He was a 23-year-old farmer when he enlisted at Louisville on October 10, 1873. Woods was assigned to Company B in the all black 9th U.S. Cavalry.

On August 19, 1881, a detachment of 17 troopers from Company B, 9th U.S. Cavalry, under the command of 2nd Lieutenant George W. Smith, was in pursuit of Nana and his Apache raiders. The troopers were joined by a group of 20 miners led by George Daly. Nana's Apaches had attacked the miners' camp. Daly assembled a group of 20 miners, all of whom claimed to be former soldiers, and set out in pursuit. The trail led to Gavilan Canyon where Lieutenant Smith, fearing an ambush, halted his men. Daly, however, with more courage than brains, led his men into the canyon. Not willing to allow the civilians to go in alone, Lieutenant Smith relented and the troopers followed the miners into the canyon as well.

This time, it was Nana who was outnumbered, but Nana was a master at ambush and his warriors were well placed. The first that the troopers and the civilians knew of the ambush was when they came under a murderous fire from the Apache warriors. Daly, for all his rash courage, was killed in the first volley. Lieutenant Smith ordered the soldiers and civilians to dismount, but a second later a bullet slammed into his chest and Lieutenant Smith was dead. With Daly and Smith dead, the miners panicked. The order to dismount was repeated in a clear voice by Sergeant Brent Woods who, upon the death of Lieutenant Smith, was in command.

Sergeant Woods was equal to the task. He rallied the troopers and organized the civilians where they could provide a covering fire. Sergeant Woods then led the troopers in a charge against the Apaches on one side of the canyon. The remainder of the troopers were quickly pinned down by the Apaches' gunfire, but Sergeant Woods kept right on moving. He became a one-man assault force as he fought his way up the ridge. A small force of Apaches attacked Woods from the right and a bullet grazed his arm, but Woods held his ground, shooting at his attackers as fast as he could until they were driven off. The Indians finally broke under the pressure and abandoned their positions.

Nana, however, again had accomplished his goal. With their dead and wounded, the white men would no longer follow him. Nana broke off the attack and escaped into Mexico.

Sergeant Brent Woods was awarded the Medal of Honor for saving the lives of his comrades and the civilians at Gavilan Canyon. His courage under fire was summed up by one of the civilians: "That Sergeant Woods is an S.O.B. in a fight. If it hadn't been for him, none of us would have come out of that canyon."

Brent Woods was discharged from the service in 1902. Woods and his wife, Pearl, returned to Pulaski County, Kentucky, where he died in the spring of 1906. He was only 54.

Chapter 3

Peacetime from
1872 to 1890

As a general rule, the Medal of Honor may be awarded for deeds of personal bravery or self-sacrifice above and beyond the call of duty only while the person is a member of the Armed Forces of the United States in action against an enemy of the United States. However, until the passage of Public Law 88-77, the Navy could and did award Medals of Honor for bravery in the line of the naval profession. Such awards recognized bravery in saving life, and deeds of valor performed in submarine rescues, boiler explosions, turret fires, and other types of disaster unique to the naval profession.

The eight African Americans who earned the Navy's Medal of Honor between 1872 and 1890 are, for the most part, lost and forgotten heroes. Each earned the Medal of Honor for risking his life in the attempt to save the life of a comrade. Yet in only two of the cases, those of Daniel Atkins and Robert Sweeney, is anything significant known about the men who performed these deeds of valor.

Robert Sweeney is just one of 18 men in the history of the United States to have earned two Medals of Honor. In 1918, the Regulations on Awards were changed to read, "...that not more than one Medal of Honor could be awarded to any one individual." Since the law has changed to prohibit the award of a second Medal of Honor, this is a small and distinguished group that will never get any larger. Of the 18 men with two Medals of Honor, five were U.S. Marines fighting with Army units during World War I who earned both the Army and the Navy Medal of

Honor for the same deed. Only 13 men have two Medals of Honor for two separate deeds. Robert Sweeney is one of this select group.

Almost nothing, other than their name and a one or two line description of their deed, is known about the six other African Americans who received the Medal of Honor during this period. They each served their time in the Navy, earned a Medal of Honor for their courage, and then disappeared in history and were lost. It is hoped that the publication of this book may bring to light additional details concerning the lives of these great men.

Ship's Cook Daniel Atkins, USN

U.S.S. Cushing

Daniel Atkins was born on November 18, 1866, at Brunswick, Virginia. Atkins enlisted in the U.S. Navy in Virginia and was assigned to the U.S.S. Cushing.

Ship's Cook Atkins earned the Medal of Honor on February 11, 1898, while serving aboard the U.S.S. Cushing. His citation reads as follows: "On board the U.S.S. Cushing, February 11, 1898. Showing gallant conduct, Atkins attempted to save the life of the late Ensign Joseph C. Breckenridge, U.S. Navy, who fell overboard at sea from that vessel on this date."

The U.S.S. Cushing was steaming for Havana, Cuba, through very rough seas. Men have to eat even in bad weather, so Atkins was in the ship's galley going about his business. Up on the deck, Ensign Joseph C. Breckenridge was on his way to his quarters when a giant wave swept over the deck. The wave swept everything that was not tied down, including Ensign Breckenridge, overboard.

"Man overboard," a sailor yelled. "Man overboard," others took up the cry of alarm. From the Cushing's railing, Ensign Breckenridge could be seen struggling in the water, as the violent waves threw him around like a rag doll. One seaman threw Breckenridge a lifeline but the surging waves carried it away from the drowning man.

Lieutenant Albert Gleaves, the Cushing's commander, ordered the engines stopped and the helm to port. When the engines were stopped, John Everetts and Frank Cappage threw life preservers to Breckenridge but they fell short. Lieutenant Gleaves then ordered the starboard lifeboat be lowered. With Everetts and Cappage aboard, the lifeboat was lowered into the ocean but the huge waves immediately swamped the boat. Everetts and Cappage had to be pulled back aboard the *Cushing*.

By this time, it was clear that Ensign Breckenridge had been overcome and his body was drifting away from the ship. Lieutenant Gleaves ordered the *Cushing* to be brought closer to the body. Once the *Cushing* had been maneuvered as close to Breckenridge's body as possible, Everett dove from the forecastle with a lifeline to be secured to the dead officer. Everetts, however, was soon in trouble himself. One giant wave after another crashed down upon him, causing Everetts to panic. It appeared that Everetts, too, was to become a victim of the sea.

At this critical point, Ship's Cook Atkins removed his shoes and outer garments and, taking a lifeline, dove into the ocean. Atkins was not an accomplished swimmer but he demonstrated a cool courage in the face of danger. In the surging ocean more than swimming skills were necessary. The ability not to panic in face of the giant waves was just as crucial. The crew of the *Cushing*, standing along the rails, watched Atkins swim out towards the dead officer and the now floundering Everetts. The sea was cold and huge waves threw Atkins about. The valiant little cook kept his composure and swam on. Once Atkins reached Everetts, he had another problem. Everetts was in a frantic state of panic, fighting and kicking Atkins. With tremendous effort Atkins was able to fight the waves, subdue Everett and get a line attached to Breckenridge's body. All three were then pulled to the *Cushing* and safety.

Daniel Atkins died May 11, 1923, at Portsmouth, Virginia. He is buried at the U.S. Navy Hospital Cemetery, Portsmouth, Virginia.

Ordinary Seaman John Davis, USN

U.S.S. Trenton

John Davis was born in 1854 at Kingston, Jamaica. Seaman Davis was the fourth African American to earn the Medal of Honor for heroism outside of the United States. Seaman Davis earned his Medal of Honor in February 1881 while serving aboard the U.S.S. *Trenton*. The *Trenton* was at Toulon, France, when Coxswain Augustus Ohlensen fell overboard and was floundering in the water. At the risk of his own life, Seaman Davis jumped overboard to save the life of his shipmate. His simple citation reads as follows: "On board the U.S.S. *Trenton*, Toulon, France, February 1881. Jumping overboard, Davis rescued Augustus Ohlensen, coxswain, from drowning."

John Davis died August 19, 1903, at Hampton, Virginia. He is buried at Hampton National Cemetery, Hampton, Virginia.

Seaman Alphonse Girandy, USN

U.S.S. Petrel

Alphonse Girandy was born on January 21, 1868, on the island of Guadeloupe, in the West Indies. He enlisted in the U.S. Navy in Pennsylvania and was assigned to serve aboard the U.S.S. *Petrel*.

Seaman Girandy earned the Medal of Honor on March 31, 1901, for risking his own life to save the lives of his fellow sailors aboard the U.S.S. *Petrel* on the high seas. His citation reads as follows: "Serving on board the U.S.S. *Petrel*, for heroism and gallantry, fearlessly exposing his own life to danger for the saving of others, on the occasion of the fire on board that vessel, 31 March 1901."

Alphonse Girandy died on April 3, 1941. He is buried in the Philadelphia National Cemetery, Philadelphia, Pennsylvania.

Seaman John Johnson, USN

U.S.S. Kansas

John Johnson was born in 1839 at Philadelphia, Philadelphia County, Pennsylvania. He enlisted in the Navy from Pennsylvania.

Seaman John Johnson was the second African American to earn the Medal of Honor for heroism outside the United States. Seaman Johnson earned his Medal of Honor on April 12, 1872, while serving aboard the U.S.S. *Kansas* near Greytown, Nicaragua. His citation reads as follows: "Serving on board the U.S.S. *Kansas* near Greytown, Nicaragua, 12 April 1872, Johnson displayed great coolness and self-possession at the time Commander F. Crosman and others were drowned and, by extraordinary heroism and personal exertion, prevented greater loss of life."

There is a story here, but it appears to be lost in history. The citation does not tell what happened, but assumes its reader knows about the time Commander F. Crosman and the others drowned. What had happened aboard the *Kansas*?

Seaman John Johnson is equally a mystery. After his tour of duty in the Navy, he simply disappears. I have been unable to find any other details of his life.

Cooper William Johnson, USN
U.S.S. Adams

William Johnson was born in 1855 on the island of St. Vincent in the Virgin Islands. Johnson enlisted in the U.S. Navy at New York and held the rank of cooper. A cooper makes and repairs wooden containers such as barrels, casks, tubs and sometime crates. Cooper Johnson was assigned to serve aboard the U.S.S. *Adams.*

Cooper Johnson earned his Medal of Honor on November 14, 1879, aboard the U.S.S. *Adams* at the Mare Island, Navy Yard, California. Johnson, at the risk of his own life jumped into the sea to save a workman from drowning. His citation reads as follows: "Serving on board the U.S.S. *Adams* at the Navy Yard, Mare Island, California, November 14, 1879, Johnson rescued Daniel W. Kloppen, a workman, from drowning."

William Johnson died on May 20, 1903. He is buried in the Arlington National Cemetery, Arlington, Virginia, where a special headstone marks his grave as a recipient of the Medal of Honor.

Grave of Cooper William Johnson, USN

Seaman Joseph B. Noil, USN

U.S.S. Powhatan

Joseph B. Noil was born in 1841 at Nova Scotia, Canada. He enlisted in the U.S. Navy from New York and achieved the rank of Seaman. Seaman Noil was assigned to serve aboard the U.S.S. *Powhatan.*

Seaman Noil was the first African American to earn the Medal of Honor after the Civil War. Noil earned his Medal of Honor on December 26, 1872, while the *Powhatan* was anchored off Norfolk, Virginia. When Boatswain J. C. Walton fell overboard, Seaman Noil risked his own life in saving the life of his fellow sailor. His simple citation reads as follows: "Serving on board the U.S.S. *Powhatan* at Norfolk, 26 December 1872, Noil saved Boatswain J. C. Walton from drowning."

After the expiration of his enlistment Joseph B. Noil left the Navy and disappears into history. Nothing more is known about the rest of his life.

Seaman John Smith, USN

U.S.S. Shenandoah

John Smith was born in 1854 on the island of Bermuda. Smith enlisted in the U.S. Navy from New York and achieved the rank of Seaman. Seaman Smith was assigned to serve aboard the U.S.S. *Shenandoah.*

Seaman John Smith was the third African American to receive the Medal of Honor for heroism outside of the United States. Smith earned his Medal of Honor on September 19, 1880, for risking his life to save the life of Fireman James Grady who had fallen overboard. His simple citation reads as follows: "For jumping overboard from the U.S.S. *Shenandoah*, at Rio de Janeiro, Brazil, 19 September 1880, and rescuing from drowning James Grady, first class fireman."

Nothing more is known about the life of John Smith. Once he completed his tour of duty in the Navy he, like several other black recipients of the Medal of Honor, simply disappears.

Ordinary Seaman
Robert Augustus Sweeney, USN

U.S.S. Kersarge *and U.S.S.* Yanic

Earning the Medal of Honor is an extraordinary feat. From 1863 to 1997 there have been 3,457 men and one woman who have earned the highest award for valor given by their country. As extraordinary as that feat is, there are 18 men who have been awarded two Medals of Honor. Of those 18 men, five of the double recipients were U.S. Marines serving in World War I who received both the Army and the Navy Medal of Honor for a single deed of valor. That leaves 13 men who have earned two Medals of Honor for two separate deeds of valor. This is a feat which will not be duplicated, as current law allows for the award of only one Medal of Honor to an individual. One of those rare men with two Medals of Honor is Robert A. Sweeney.

Robert Augustus Sweeney was born on February 20, 1853, at Montserrat Island, West Indies. Sweeney first enlisted in the U.S. Navy for a three-year hitch from New Jersey, on December 1, 1873. Sweeney was assigned to serve aboard the U.S.S. *Vermont.* During his first two tours of duty, Sweeney served aboard the following vessels, the U.S.S. *Vermont,* the U.S.S. *Colorado,* the U.S.S. *Pawnee,* the U.S.S. *Dictator,* the U.S.S *Powhatan,* the U.S.S. *Constellation,* the U.S.S. *Powhatan,* the U.S.S. *Franklin* and the U.S.S. *Powhatan* again.

Ordinary Seaman Sweeney commenced his third enlistment on September 17, 1881. He was assigned to serve aboard the U.S.S. *Kersarge.* Sweeney earned his first Medal of Honor for saving a fellow sailor from drowning on October 26, 1881.

On October 26, 1881, the U.S.S. *Kersarge* sailed into Hampton Roads in a storm, fighting a strongly running tide. A crewman fell overboard, calling for help and yelling that he could not swim. Seaman Sweeney jumped overboard after the sailor. Once in the water, Sweeney found that the tide was almost too much for him. It nearly sucked him under several times before he reached the floundering sailor. Sweeney was able to reach the sailor, but he then had to fight the rough seas and the tide for 20 minutes until the U.S.S. *Kersarge* could reach him and fish the two men out of the water. For this heroic deed, Sweeney was awarded his first Medal of Honor.

Ordinary Seaman Sweeney transferred to the U.S.S. *Yanic* on

September 6, 1883. Three months after his transfer to the U.S.S. *Yanic,* Sweeney earned his second Medal of Honor, again for saving a fellow sailor from drowning.

On December 20, 1883, the U.S.S. *Yanic* was in the New York Navy yard tied up along-side the U.S.S. *Jamestown.* At 4:15 A.M., a cabin boy from the *Jamestown,* known as George, fell overboard from a plank going from the *Jamestown* to the *Yanic.* Seaman Sweeney from the *Yanic* and Landman J.W. Norris from the *Jamestown* saw George fall. Without hesitation, both men plunged into the ocean to save the boy. Both Sweeney and Norris received a Medal of Honor for saving the life of Cabin Boy George.

Sweeney left the Navy on June 18, 1890, at the end of his fourth tour of duty with a medical discharge, having earned two Medals of Honor. Robert Augustus Sweeney died December 19, 1890, at Bellvue Hospital, New York City, New York. He is buried in an unmarked grave in Cavalry Cemetery, Woodside, New York.

Chapter 4

The Spanish-American War (1898)

At the outbreak of the Spanish-American War, the U.S. government sent the 9th and 10th Cavalry as well as the 24th and 25th Infantry to Cuba. These African American regiments, battle hardened by their campaigns against American Indians, were among the Army's most elite units. In the Spanish-American War, these regiments lived up to their well deserved reputations. A Southern born officer, impressed with the quality of the black soldiers, stated, "They were the best, the readiest, the most cheerful, and, I believe, the deadliest fighters in the war." An officer of the 6th Infantry said, after having watched the men of the 24th in action, "Those colored fellows were the lions, afraid of nothing."

Even Theodore Roosevelt in his memoir of the war with Spain remarked several times upon the courage of the black soldiers at Las Guasimas and on the San Juan Heights. Roosevelt observed that the black soldiers did not trust officers outside of their own regiments, but, led by an officer that they trusted, "the colored troops did as well as any soldiers possibly could do."

In the war, there were always two enemies— the one you were shooting at and that would shoot back at you, and disease. Between the two, disease was often the most dangerous. During the American Civil War, the Union lost 360,000 killed and the Confederacy lost 260,000 killed. Most of those killed on both sides died from diseases, not from wounds inflicted in battle. During the Mexican-American War, a large part of General Scott's strategy was to get his soldiers away from the coast before the yellow fever season. The goal of the Mexicans was to contain the American army to the coast, where the yellow fever would decimate its ranks, saving the Mexicans the trouble of killing them.

In the Spanish-American War, the most deadly enemy was not the Spanish, but yellow fever and malaria. Immediately after the surrender of Santiago, the American army was struck with a major medical crisis. The first case of yellow fever was detected on June 6. By June 8, there were three cases, by June 11, a hundred and the number kept rising. At the same time, malaria also broke out among the troops.

On July 14, the men of the 24th Infantry, one of the Army's black regiments, volunteered to serve as nurses, it being widely believed that African Americans had a natural immunity to yellow fever. Such was, in fact, not the case. Of the 60 volunteers from the 24th who were accepted to act as nurses, 36 would eventually die themselves of malaria or yellow fever.

Soon virtually the entire army was on the sick list. Routine military tasks, such as inspections and posting of sentries, had to be suspended, as there were too few men fit for duty. In all, about 80 percent of the V Corps stationed at Santiago was stricken by either yellow fever or malaria.

On July 19, General Shafter, while refusing to admit there was a crisis, requested hundreds of medical personnel, hospital attendants, nurses and doctors, as well as two "immune regiments." As the extent of the yellow fever problem became known, the government created ten new regiments made up from black men from the South who were thought to be immune to yellow fever. The 7th, 8th, 9th and 10th U.S. Volunteers, known as "immune regiments," were raised and sent to Cuba and the Philippines. These new black regiments would perform the occupation duty for the newly acquired territories.

The raising of the immune regiments gave some black soldiers the opportunity to serve as officers. Medal of Honor recipients William McBryar and Edward L. Baker would serve as lieutenants during this time. Both men served well as officers and neither man would ever be satisfied with being a non-commissioned officer again.

In addition to black regiments in the regular Army, a number of volunteer regiments were raised, but the war ended too soon for most of the volunteers to reach the front. These black volunteer regiments included the 3rd Alabama, 1st D.C. Separate Battalion, 8th Illinois, 23rd Kansas, 3rd North Carolina, 9th Ohio and the 6th Virginia. In addition, Company L of the 6th Massachusetts was an entirely black unit. Many of the officers in these volunteer regiments were black. Only the 3rd Alabama had no black officers. On the other hand, the 8th Illinois was commanded throughout its existence by Colonel John Marshall, a prosperous black businessman.

The only black volunteers to come under fire during the Spanish-American War was Company L, of the 6th Massachusetts, which was involved in some skirmishes in a campaign in Puerto Rico.

The exact number of African Americans who served in the Spanish-American War is difficult to establish. About 5,000 men served in the 9th and 10th Cavalry and the 24th and 25th Regiments, which were regular Army regiments. Another 7,000 African Americans served in the Volunteer regiments and about 5,000 men served in the "immune regiments." A total of 17,000 men comprised 6 percent of the total Army's manpower.

The U.S. Navy also included many African Americans. Nearly 10 percent of the men in the fleet were black. Unlike the Army, the Navy was not segregated. While there were no black officers, blacks served alongside whites in all enlisted positions including such prestigious petty officer positions as chief bosun's mate and chief gunner's mate. In the Revenue Cutter Service—the precursor to the Coast Guard—blacks served as both enlisted men and as officers, including some ship's captains.

Five African American soldiers earned the Medal of Honor during the Spanish-American War. The stories of their courage and valor follow.

Sergeant Edward L. Baker, Jr., USA

10th U.S. Cavalry

Edward Lee Baker, Jr., was born on December 28, 1865, at Platte River, Laramie County, Wyoming. Baker was born in a freight wagon, while his family was en route to California. His father was French and his mother was African American. Baker enlisted as a private in the 9th U.S. Cavalry on July 7, 1882, at Cincinnati, Ohio.

Baker served in the Army for 28 years, participating in the Indian Wars, the Spanish-American War and the Philippines Insurrection. By 1898, Baker had been promoted to sergeant major and was serving with the 10th U.S. Cavalry in Cuba.

Sergeant Baker earned the Medal of Honor on July 1, 1898, at Santiago, Cuba. For those who lived during the Spanish-American War, the date July 1, 1898, would tell the whole story. It is like mentioning December 7, 1941 (Peal Harbor Day), to a later generation. For July 1, 1898, was the date that U.S. forces stormed up San Juan Hill in Cuba.

At dawn on July 1st General Wheeler's division of dismounted cavalry was camped on the eminence of El Poso, the name of a ruined plantation about three miles from Santiago. Kent's division lay near the road back of El Poso. It had been arranged the previous night that while Lawton turned northward to attack El Caney, there should be a general movement of the rest of the army towards Santiago. The cavalry division was to cross the Aguadores River and deploy to the right along the base of San Juan Hill, where the Spanish were strongly entrenched. The troops under General Kent were deployed to the left of the Spanish position.

Soon after sunrise, Grimes' battery went into position a little way west of the ruined buildings of El Poso, prepared gun pits and opened fire on San Juan Hill. Firing, promptly answered by the enemy with shrapnel, continued for an hour or more and then Wheeler's division was put in march towards Santiago. Under the direction of General Sumner, who held temporary command due to the illness of General Wheeler, the division crossed the Aguadores, turned to the right in the face of a galling volley of fire from the enemy and went into position. Kent's division followed Wheeler's across the stream, advanced in close order under a severe enfilading fire, turned off to the left and formed for the attack.

Kent's advance, though skillfully directed, was not accomplished without heavy loss. The enemy infantry fire, steadily increasing in intensity, came from all directions not only from the front and the dense tropical thickets on the American's flanks, but from Spanish sharpshooters thickly posted in trees to the Americans' rear. While the Third Brigade, consisting of the 9th, 13th and 24th Infantry, was deploying into position, its commander Colonel Wikoff was killed. Command of the brigade devolved upon Lieutenant-Colonel Worth, who immediately fell severely wounded, and then upon Lieutenant-Colonel Liscum. Five minutes later Liscum also fell under the enemy's withering fire and Lieutenant-Colonel Evers was left in command of the brigade. The brigade had four commanders in 11 minutes.

Once in place the Third Brigade of Wheeler's Division had begun and carried out the most desperate and heroic charge of the war. The object of the charge was a block house on the top of San Juan Hill, guarded by trenches and other defenses a mile and a half long. In preparing their defenses the Spanish had made extensive use of barbed wire fencing, which proved most effective as a stop to the American advance. It was used in two ways. Wire was stretched near the ground to trip up the American soldiers when on the run. Beyond them were fences of barbed wire too high to be vaulted over. The wires were braided in such a way that they had to be separated before an ordinary wire cutter could be forced between them. Every fence required a temporary halt on the part of the charging American forces and during those moments they were exposed to a pitiless fire from all sides.

The most effective defenses of San Juan Hill, however, were the steep side of the hill and the rifle pits surmounting them. It seemed almost incredible that the Americans could have scaled those heights under fire from rapid loading magazine guns. But they did. It was a moment pregnant with heroism. It was delivered of thousands of heroes, one of whom by his conspicuous rank, his intrepid coolness and magnetic control of men stood out among them all. General Henry S. Hawkins rode out in front of his regiments and scornfully turning his back on the Spanish line and cried: "Boys, the time has come. Every man who loves his country, forward and follow me!"

General Hawkins turned his horse and with set face road forward up the hill. Two thousand American soldiers rose to their feet with a tremendous cheer in which the "Rebel yell" and the Indian yell were mingled. The soldiers dashed up the hill after their fearless leader. General Hawkins urged his men forward and led them through a zone of most destructive fire and up the steep and difficult hill. The 6th, 16th, 13th, and 24th Infantry charged up the hill.

Through volley after volley of withering fire, during which men reeled and fell out while their unhurt comrades filled the gaps and closed ranks, the Americans climbed and pulled themselves up the hill until they could see the strained and amazed eyes of the Spanish gazing at a spectacle they had never witnessed before — the dogged advance of the intrepid Americans who would not be denied by even the yawning hell that modern instruments of war could belch in their faces.

The regiments that suffered the heaviest casualties were the 13th and the 24th. It was 75 men of the 24th Infantry under the command of Captain Ducat and Lieutenant Lyon that made the final charge to capture the blockhouse. Of the 75 men who made the final charge, more than half were killed or wounded. Ducat's troops fired as they ran, rushing up the hill in a storm of bullets. Neither Captain Ducat or Lieutenant Lyon reached the blockhouse, both falling wounded on the slope; but such was the determination of their men that they completed the charge even without an officer to lead them. The Spaniards, dismayed that the Americans just kept coming against all the firepower, retreated from the blockhouse, leaving it to Ducat's men.

At the same time that General Hawkins' brigade was attacking up the hill, General Wheeler's dismounted cavalry with the Tenth and the Rough Riders in the lead had charged up San Juan Hill on the right, arriving at the crest at about the same time as the infantry did. Lieutenant-Colonel Roosevelt road at the head of the Rough Riders, mounted high on horseback and charging the rifle pits at a gallop.

General Hawkins and Lieutenant-Colonel Roosevelt were the two officers most conspicuous in the taking of San Juan Hill, but it is folly to claim that any two men, or any one man was more brave or daring or showed greater courage in that slow stubborn advance than did any of the others.

Attacking up San Juan Hill with the 10th Cavalry of Wheeler's division was Sergeant-Major Edward L. Baker. Surrounded by acts of bravery and daring on all sides, never the less Sergeant Baker's deeds singled him out to receive a Medal of Honor. His simple citation reads as follows: "Left cover and, under fire, rescued a wounded comrade from drowning" (the wounded man had been shot while attempting to cross a river at the base of the hill).

After his service in Cuba, Baker was promoted to lieutenant and then to captain. He held positions in both the 10th U.S. Infantry and the 24th U.S. Infantry. Captain Baker commanded a Company of the 24th Infantry during the Philippine Insurrection.

Following his mustering out from the 24th, Baker returned to the Philippines and served with the Philippine Scouts. He retired a Captain of the Philippine Scouts in 1909.

Edward Lee Baker, Jr., died August 26, 1913, at the Presidio of San Francisco, California. He is buried at Rosedale Cemetery, Los Angeles, California.

Private Dennis Bell, USA

10th U.S. Cavalry

Dennis Bell was born on December 28, 1866, in Washington, D.C. Bell enlisted in the Army at Washington, D.C., and was assigned to Troop H, 10th U.S. Cavalry.

Private Dennis Bell earned the Medal of Honor on June 30, 1898, at Tayabacoa, Cuba. His citation reads as follows: "Voluntarily went ashore in the face of the enemy and aided in the rescue of his wounded comrades; this after several previous attempts at rescue had been frustrated."

On June 30, 1898, units of the 10th Cavalry, aboard the U.S.S. *Florida*, attempted a landing at Tayabacoa on the east coast of Cuba to link up with Cuban insurgent forces under General Gomes. Unfortunately, the landing was affected only a few hundred yards from a blockhouse where a Spanish garrison was posted. Shortly after the landing, the U.S. forces were ambushed and the majority of troops abandoned the beachhead, leaving behind at least 16 wounded comrades, who were taken prisoner by the Spaniards.

Back aboard the U.S.S. *Florida*, a call for volunteers to rescue the 16 men was made. After a number of unsuccessful rescue attempts had been made by others, Private George H. Wanton, Private Dennis Bell, Private Fitz Lee and Private William H. Thompkins stepped forward and volunteered for the assignment of recovering the prisoners. Putting ashore in a launch, Wanton and his men surprised the Spanish forces holding the prisoners in a stockade and secured their release. Bell and his men, together with the freed prisoners, were all able to return safely the ship.

For this deed, privates Dennis Bell, Fitz Lee, William H. Thompkins and George Henry Wanton were all awarded the Medal of Honor on June 23, 1899.

Dennis Bell died on September 25, 1953, at Washington, D.C. He is buried at Arlington National Cemetery, Arlington, Virginia, where a special headstone marks his grave as a recipient of the Medal of Honor.

Grave of Private Dennis Bell, USA

Private Fitz Lee

10th U.S. Cavalry

Fitz Lee was born in June 1866, in Dinwiddie County, Virginia. Lee enlisted in Troop M, 10th U.S. Cavalry, at Philadelphia, Pennsylvania.

Private Lee earned the Medal of Honor on June 30, 1898, at Tayabacoa, Cuba. His citation reads as follows: "Voluntarily went ashore in the face of the enemy and aided in the rescue of his wounded comrades; this after several previous attempts had been frustrated."

On June 30, 1898, units of the 10th Cavalry, aboard the U.S.S. *Florida,* attempted a landing at Tayabacoa on the east coast of Cuba to link up with Cuban insurgent forces under General Gomes. Shortly after the landing, the U.S. forces were ambushed and the majority of troops abandoned the beachhead, leaving behind at least 16 wounded comrades, who were taken prisoner by the Spaniards.

Grave of Private Fitz Lee, USA

After several unsuccessful attempts at saving the men, Private Wanton, Private Dennis Bell, Private Fitz Lee and Private William H. Thompkins stepped forward and volunteered for the assignment of recovering the prisoners. Putting ashore in a launch, Wanton and his men surprised the Spanish forces holding the prisoners in a stockade and secured their release.

For this deed, privates Dennis Bell, Fitz Lee, William H. Thompkins and George Henry Wanton were all awarded the Medal of Honor on June 23, 1899.

A few weeks after receiving the Medal of Honor, Private Lee was suffering from an illness which caused him to lose his sight. Lee was discharged at Fort

Bliss, Texas. Lee had no pension, no savings and no prospect for a job. He traveled to Fort Leavenworth, Kansas, to be with some of his old comrades who had retired and were living in the area of Fort Worth. His comrades took him in and ministered to his illness. Private Fitz Lee died at the home of a friend on September 14, 1899. He is buried at the Leavenworth National Cemetery, Leavenworth, Kansas, where a special headstone marks his grave as the final resting place of a Medal of Honor recipient.

Fireman First Class Robert Penn, USN

U.S.S. Iowa

Robert Penn was born on October 10, 1872, at Point City, Virginia. As a young man Penn worked on the farm and received very little education. Penn decided to enlist in the Navy for "a better life."

Fireman First Class Penn earned the Medal of Honor on July 20, 1898, off Santiago, Cuba. Shortly before 7:00 A.M., there was an explosion in the boiler room. Fireman Penn, who was stationed in a compartment next to the boiler room, rushed to the scene of the accident. A manhole gasket had blown off of one of the boilers. The floor of the boiler room was covered with boiling water and the air was filled with scalding steam. Penn saw a coal passer dazed and about to fall into the boiling water. Fireman Penn immediately went to the man's aid. The coal passer had badly scalded both of his feet and had a wound on his forehead. Fireman Penn managed to get to the man and carry him through the boiling water to safety.

While the coal passer was receiving treatment, Fireman Penn returned to the boiler room. The coals from the fire were spilling out of the damaged furnace and threatened to create another explosion. Quickly, Fireman Penn created a bridge over the boiling water by placing a plank between two ash buckets. The improvised bridge was just one foot above the boiling water. Penn crossed the bridge with a fire shovel and got a load of flaming coals and transported them to a safe place. Back and forth across his makeshift bridge Penn went, braving the heat and the steam taking load after of live coals to a safe place.

Fireman Penn was awarded the Medal of Honor for his efforts to save his ship at the risk of his own life. His citation reads as follows:

On board the U.S.S. *Iowa* off Santiago de Cuba, 20 July 1898. Performing his duty at the risk of serious scalding at the time of the blowing out of the manhole gasket on board the vessel, Penn hauled the fire while standing on a board thrown across a coal bucket 1 foot above the boiling water which was still blowing from the boiler.

Robert Penn died on June 8, 1912, at Las Animas, Colorado. He is buried at an unknown cemetery in Philadelphia, Pennsylvania.

Private William H. Thompkins, USA

10th U.S. Cavalry

William H. Thompkins was born October 3, 1872, at Paterson, Passaic County, New Jersey. Thompkins enlisted in the Army at Paterson, New Jersey, and was assigned to Troop G, 10th U.S. Cavalry.

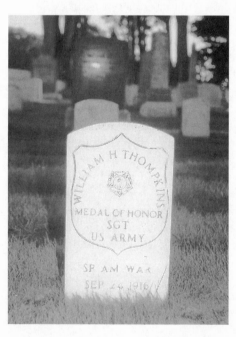

Private Thompkins earned the Medal of Honor on June 30, 1898, at Tayabacoa, Cuba. His citation reads as follows: "Voluntarily went ashore in the face of the enemy and aided in the rescue of his wounded comrades; this after several previous attempts at rescue had been frustrated."

On June 30, 1898, units of the 10th Cavalry, aboard the U.S.S. *Florida*, attempted a landing at Tayabacoa on the east coast of Cuba to link up with Cuban insurgent forces under General Gomes. Unfortunately, the landing was affected only a few hundred yards from a blockhouse where a Spanish garrison was posted. Shortly after the landing, the U.S. forces were ambushed and the majority of troops

Grave of Private William H. Thompkins, USA

abandoned the beachhead, leaving behind at least 16 wounded comrades, who were taken prisoner by the Spaniards.

After several unsuccessful attempts at saving the men had been made by others, Private Wanton, Private Dennis Bell, Private Fitz Lee and Private William H. Thompkins stepped forward and volunteered for the assignment of recovering the prisoners. Putting ashore in a launch, Thompkins and his men surprised the Spanish forces holding the prisoners in a stockade and secured their release.

For this deed, privates Dennis Bell, Fitz Lee, William H. Thompkins and George Henry Wanton were all awarded the Medal of Honor on June 23, 1899.

William H. Thompkins died September 24, 1916. He is buried in the San Francisco National Cemetery, San Francisco, California.

Private George Henry Wanton, USA

10th U.S. Cavalry

George Henry Wanton was born on May 15, 1866, at Paterson, Passaic County, New Jersey. The son of William H. Wanton and Margaret (Miller) Wanton, George Wanton attended public schools in Paterson before enlisting in the U.S. Navy in 1884. Wanton served a four year enlistment and was discharged in 1888.

In 1889, Wanton enlisted at Paterson, in Troop M, 10th U.S. Cavalry. In 1892, Wanton received a promotion to corporal but had been demoted back to his rank as private when he earned the Medal of Honor.

Private Wanton earned the Medal of Honor on June 30, 1898, at Tayabacoa, Cuba. His citation reads as follows: "Voluntarily went ashore in the face of the enemy and aided in the rescue of his wounded comrades; this after several previous attempts at rescue had been frustrated."

On June 30, 1898, units of the 10th Cavalry, aboard the U.S.S. *Florida*, attempted a landing at Tayabacoa on the east coast of Cuba to link up with up with Cuban insurgent forces under General Gomes. Shortly after the landing, the U.S. forces were ambushed and the majority of troops abandoned the beachhead, leaving behind at least 16 wounded comrades, who were taken prisoner by the Spaniards.

After several unsuccessful attempts at saving the men had been made by others, Private Wanton, Private Dennis Bell, Private Fitz Lee

Grave of Private George Henry Wanton, USA

and Private William H. Thompkins stepped forward and volunteered for the assignment of recovering the prisoners. Putting ashore in a launch, Wanton and his men surprised the Spanish forces holding the prisoners in a stockade and secured their release.

For this deed, privates Dennis Bell, Fitz Lee, William H. Thompkins and George Henry Wanton were all awarded the Medal of Honor on June 23, 1899.

Wanton was promoted to sergeant in 1898 and served the remainder of his Army career with the 10th Cavalry. Sergeant Wanton retired from the service in 1925. He was invited to visit Washington and act as an Honorary Pall Bearer at the burial of the Unknown Soldier of World War I in the Memorial Amphitheater at the Arlington National Cemetery in 1921.

George Henry Wanton died on November 27, 1940, at Walter Reed Hospital in Washington D.C. He was buried with full military honors in Arlington National Cemetery, Arlington, Virginia.

Chapter 5

World War I
(1914–1918)

When the U.S. 369th Infantry Regiment landed in France early in 1918, no division in the American Expeditionary Force wanted it because its soldiers were black. Eventually, General John J. Pershing sloughed off the unit to the French Fourth Army. The commander of the 369th, Colonel William Hayward, told a friend, "Our great American general simply put the black orphan in a basket, set it on the door of the French, pulled the bell and went away."

Altogether during World War I, 370,000 African Americans enlisted or were drafted into the armed forces. More than half of these men were assigned to the all black 92nd and 93rd Infantry Divisions. While the black 92nd Division did fight alongside other American units, the 93rd Division was primarily brigaded with French troops.

The French, accustomed to troops from their African colonies, welcomed the reinforcements. The 369th Infantry, along with the three other regiments of the 92nd Division, fought alongside the French with distinction. The French issued a unit *Croix de Guerre* to three regiments and one company.

Black soldiers participated in the battles of Argonne Forest, Château-Thierry, St. Mihiel, Champagne, Voges and Metz. The French appreciated the fighting quality of the black troops. One hundred seventy-one African American soldiers earned the French *Croix de Guerre* for their courage on the battlefield.

The vast majority of black soldiers, however, were not on the

119

battlefields. They were assigned to service units, including quartermaster and transportation. Some black soldiers were even assigned as stevedores on the French docks. These assignments only served to enforce the stereotype that black soldiers could not or would not fight and were only good for non-combat service roles.

When properly trained and allowed to fight, black soldiers made extraordinarily good warriors. The all black 369th Infantry Regiment (the "Hell Fighters") was an outstanding unit. It was in continuous combat longer than any other American unit in World War I, and it was the first allied regiment to fight its way to the Rhine River in the final offensive against Germany. The all black 370th, 371st and 372nd Infantry Regiments also compiled outstanding service records.

In World War I, black soldiers worked, fought and died to preserve freedom in strictly segregated units. Promotions for black soldiers were rare. Only about 1,400 African Americans were commissioned as officers in the Army. The highest ranking African American was a colonel. There were no African Americans commissioned as officers in the Navy.

While several black soldiers were awarded the Distinguished Service Cross, the Army's second highest medal for valor, not one of the African Americans who fought in World War I was awarded the Medal of Honor. As time passed, it became clear that, considering the record of the black soldiers, this could only have been the result of racial prejudice.

In 1988, the Army, under pressure from critics, launched an investigation into why no black soldiers had been awarded the highest award for valor, the Medal of Honor. All of the recommendations for awards for black soldiers were reviewed. The research showed that four African Americans had been recommended for the Medal of Honor for their courage on the battlefields of Europe. Three of the four recommendations had been subsequently downgraded to the Distinguished Service Cross and the black soldiers involved had received that medal. The investigation also found that one of the four black soldiers recommended for the Medal of Honor had never received any award at all. Corporal Freddie Stowers, for his gallantry on September 28, 1918, at Hill 188, had been originally recommended for a Distinguished Service Cross. In the normal review process, the recommendation had been upgraded to the Medal of Honor. Then, for some unexplained reason, the matter was dropped and no action was ever taken on either recommendation.

The recommendations for Corporal Freddie Stowers had simply dropped through the cracks. Here was a way for the Army to pull out of its dilemma. It could pacify its critics and award a black soldier the Medal of Honor without really admitting the racial prejudice, which had kept him and at least some of his brothers from being awarded the Medal of Honor in the first place.

On April 24, 1991, seventy-two years after he died attacking German machine-gun nests in France, Corporal Freddie Stowers was awarded the Medal of Honor by President George Bush in a special ceremony at the White House. The medal was presented to Corporal Stowers' surviving sisters. While there is no question that Corporal Stowers deserved the medal, in a very real way the award not only recognized his courage and valor, but also that of hundreds of his brothers in arms whose deeds of courage and self sacrifice were never so honored — not because their deeds did not merit recognition but because they were black.

Corporal Freddie Stowers, USA

371st U.S. Infantry

Freddie Stowers was born in 1896 in Anderson County, South Carolina. Freddie worked on the family farm growing cotton and "anything else that would grow." In October 1917, Stowers enlisted in the Army at Anderson County, South Carolina. He was assigned to Company C, 1st Battalion, 371st Infantry, an all black unit organized at Camp Jackson, South Carolina. The regiment became part of the all black 93rd Infantry Division.

Corporal Stowers earned the Medal of Honor on September 28, 1918, at Hill 188, Champagne, Marne Sector, France. His citation reads as follows:

> Corporal Stowers, a native of Anderson County, South Carolina, distinguished himself by exceptional heroism on 28 September 1918, while serving as a squad leader in Company C, 371st Infantry Regiment, 93rd Infantry Division. His company was the lead company during the attack on Hill 188, Champagne Marne Sector, France, during World War I. A few minutes after the attack began, the enemy ceased firing and began climbing up onto the parapets of the trenches, holding up their arms as if wishing to surrender. The enemy's actions caused the American forces to cease fire and to come

out into the open. As the company started forward and when within about 100 meters of the trench line, the enemy jumped back into their trenches and greeted Corporal Stowers' company with interlocking bands of machine gun fire and mortar fire causing well over fifty percent casualties. Faced with incredible enemy resistance, Corporal Stowers took charge, setting such a courageous example of personal bravery and leadership that he inspired his men to follow him in the attack. With extraordinary heroism and complete disregard of personal danger under devastating fire, he crawled forward leading his squad toward an enemy machine gun nest, which was causing heavy casualties to his company. After fierce fighting, the machine gun position was destroyed and the enemy soldiers were killed. Displaying great courage and intrepidity, Corporal Stowers continued to press the attack against a determined enemy. While crawling forward and urging his men to continue the attack on a second trench line, he was gravely wounded by machine gun fire. Although Corporal Stowers was mortally wounded, he pressed forward, urging on the members of his squad, until he died. Inspired by the heroism and display of bravery of Corporal Stowers, his company continued the attack against incredible odds, contributing to the capture of Hill 188 and causing heavy enemy casualties. Corporal Stowers' conspicuous gallantry, extraordinary heroism and supreme devotion to his men were well above and beyond the call of duty, follow the finest traditions of military service and reflect the utmost credit on him and the United States Army.

Freddie Stowers was killed in action on September 28, 1918. He is buried at the A.B.M.C. Meuse-Argonne Cemetery, Meuse, France.

Though Stowers was denied the Medal of Honor for years because of his race, President George Bush, during ceremonies at the White House on April 24, 1991, finally corrected the injustice and awarded the Medal of Honor to Freddie Stowers' surviving sisters, 72 years after he died attacking German machine-gun nests in France.

Chapter 6

World War II
(1941–1945)

About 1.2 million African Americans served in the armed forces during World War II. Approximately 1,035,000 served in the Army and about 165,000 African Americans served in the Navy. African American soldiers and sailors served in all theaters. Due to racist stereotypes held at that time that blacks were mentally inferior and lacked the ability to operate tanks and other modern weapons, African Americans were confined mostly in the service corps, quartermaster, engineer, ordnance and transportation units.

There were, however, several all black tank and infantry units. Most of these were commanded by white officers. The largest all black unit in Europe was the 92nd Infantry Division, known as the Buffalo Division because of the term given to black soldiers during the American Indian Wars.

During the war, African Americans served in segregated units and mostly in non-combat roles. Segregation was enforced throughout the war at all military posts, in theaters, mess halls, living areas, transportation and other facilities. The Army made sure that its segregation rules were strictly enforced. A young Lieutenant Jackie Robinson was court-martialed and kicked out of the Army when he refused to give up his seat on a bus to a white soldier.

While there was still discrimination in the promotion of African Americans, some progress was being made and black junior officers became a common sight.

In both Europe and the Pacific, black soldiers, when they were allowed to fight, proved their mettle. Many African Americans were awarded the Distinguished Service Cross for their courage and self sacrifice, but again, black soldiers were passed over when it came to the highest award for valor. Of the 432 Medals of Honor bestowed during World War II, not one was awarded to an African American.

Pressured by its critics, in 1992 the U.S. Army gave Shaw University in Raleigh, North Carolina, a $600,000 grant to study whether African American soldiers had been discriminated against regarding the awarding of Medals of Honor during World War II. All the recommendations for awards to black soldiers were carefully reviewed. The result of the four-year study was a 272 page report. It concluded that, while not finding any evidence of discrimination, 10 African Americans who had been awarded the Distinguished Service Cross, but for their race, would have received the Medal of Honor. The report was clearly a political compromise which tried to walk a very fine line.

The Army's own investigation reduced the number of African Americans recommended for the Medal of Honor from ten to eight. Congress then passed a law which waived the statute of limitations, which had run out in 1952. One of the recommendations seems to have fallen through the cracks. On January 13, 1997, President William Clinton redressed a long-standing injustice and awarded the Medal of Honor to the seven outstanding black soldiers whose stories follow.

2nd Lieutenant Vernon J. Baker, USA

370th U.S. Infantry

Vernon Baker was born on December 17, 1919, at Cheyenne, Wyoming. Baker graduated in 1939 from Clarinda High School in Clarinda, Iowa. He enlisted in the Army on September 26, 1941, at Cheyenne Wyoming.

After receiving officer training Baker, on January 11, 1943, became a 25-year-old "90 day wonder" 2nd Lieutenant and was assigned to Company C, 370th Infantry Regiment, 92nd Division. The men in Baker's platoon were black men mostly in their 30s. More than a third of the men were illiterate to the point of being unable to write their own names or reading orders. They thought that the green 2nd Lieutenant was an "uppity nigger," and fought him all the way to Italy before they decided to fight Germans along with him.

Second Lieutenant Vernon Baker earned the Medal of Honor on April 5, 1945, near Viareggio, Italy. His citation reads as follows:

> For extraordinary heroism in action on 5 and 6 April 1945, near Viareggio, Italy. Then Second Lieutenant Baker demonstrated outstanding courage and leadership in destroying enemy installations, personnel and equipment during his company's attack against a strongly entrenched enemy in mountainous terrain. When his company was stopped by the concentration of fire from several machine gun emplacements, he crawled to one position and destroyed it, killing three Germans. Continuing forward, he attacked an enemy observation post and killed two occupants. With the aid of one of his men, Lieutenant Baker attacked two more machine gun nests, killing or wounding the four enemy soldiers occupying these positions. He then covered the evacuation of the wounded personnel of his company by occupying an exposed position and drawing the enemy's fire. On the following night Lieutenant Baker voluntarily led a battalion advance through enemy mine fields and heavy fire toward the division objective. Second Lieutenant Baker's fighting spirit and daring leadership were an inspiration to his men and exemplify the highest traditions of the Armed Forces.

After an intense artillery barrage, Baker led a 25-man platoon up Hill X toward the entrenched German positions in Aghinolfi Castle. Two hundred fifty yards from the castle, the platoon was pinned down by enemy fire. Lieutenant Baker saw a telescope pointing out of a slit in a bunker at the edge of the hill. Baker crawled forward to the opening, poked his M-1 into the opening and fired. When he looked inside, he found two dead Germans.

Baker next found a camouflaged machine-gun nest and attacked it, killing two more Germans. As he conferred with his company commander, Captain John Runyon, another German appeared and threw a "potato masher" grenade at the two officers. The grenade hit Captain Runyon in the helmet but failed to explode. Baker shot and killed the German who had thrown the grenade.

Baker entered the canyon alone and blasted open the hidden entrance of another dugout with a grenade, and then dashed inside and killed two more Germans with a submachine gun he had found.

Baker's own men on the hill were taking a beating. Captain Runyon, despite Lieutenant Baker's protests, ordered the platoon to withdraw. Runyon then told Baker that he was going for reinforcements. The reinforcements did not come and Lieutenant Baker never saw Captain Runyon again. Runyon made it back to the base of the hill and reported to Colonel Murphy that the platoon had been wiped out. Runyon's superior officers recommended him for a Medal of Honor, which, however, was not approved.

Lieutenant Baker covered the evacuation of the wounded personnel of his company by occupying an exposed position and drawing the enemy's fire. Only seven men of the 25 that went up the hill survived. The platoon, however, killed 26 Germans, destroyed six machine-gun nests, two observer posts and four dugouts.

On the following night, Lieutenant Baker voluntarily led a battalion advance through an enemy minefield and heavy fire to the division objective.

Lieutenant Baker was given the Distinguished Service Cross for his bravery in Italy. On January 13, 1997, after an investigation by the Army, the award was upgraded and Vernon Baker was presented with the Medal of Honor. In addition to the Medal of Honor, Baker has a Bronze Star and a Purple Heart.

After the war, Lieutenant Baker spent two years stationed in Italy. After his discharge, Baker found it hard to find a job, so he reenlisted in the Army. Baker retired in 1968 after 28 years of service. After his retirement from the Army, Baker worked for the Red Cross in California. In 1969, the Red Cross sent Baker to Vietnam for six months. After 11 years with the Red Cross, Baker retired again and lives in St Maries, Idaho.

Sergeant Edward A. Carter, Jr., USA

56th Armored Infantry

Edward Allen Carter, Jr., was born on May 26, 1916, at Los Angeles, California. He entered the service on September 26, 1941.

Sergeant Edward A. Carter earned the Medal of Honor on March 23, 1945, near Speyer, Germany.

On March 23, 1945, Sergeant Carter and his rifle squad were on a tank advancing towards Speyer, Germany. When the tank on which he was riding received heavy bazooka and small arms fire from a large warehouse, Sergeant Carter voluntarily attempted to lead a three-man group across 150 yards of open field to check out the warehouse. The attempt to cross the field was met with heavy small arms fire. Within a short time, one of his men was killed and Carter ordered the other two to pull back and provide covering fire. The fire from the warehouse was so intense that one of the two remaining men was killed and the other seriously wounded before they could take cover. Continuing on alone, Sergeant Carter was hit three times in his left leg, once in the arm and one bullet went through his hand. He was finally forced to take cover behind an earthen berm just outside the warehouse. About two hours later, eight enemy riflemen attempted to capture him. Sergeant Carter killed six of them and captured the remaining two. He then crossed the field using as a shield his two prisoners.

Sergeant Carter was awarded the Distinguished Service Cross for his valor. Although 1.2 million African Americans served in the military during World War II, none were among the 433 recipients of the Medal of Honor.

Sergeant Carter survived the war and was discharged on September 20, 1945. He died on January 30, 1963, and was buried in the Veterans Cemetery in Westwood, California.

In 1993, the Secretary of the Army, sensitive to claims the black soldiers were denied the Medal of Honor solely based upon their color, authorized a study of all of the awards given to black soldiers during World War II. The study concluded that ten black soldiers who were awarded the Distinguished Service Cross should have been given the Medal of Honor. After further investigation by the Army, on January 13, 1997, seven black soldiers, including Edward A. Carter, were

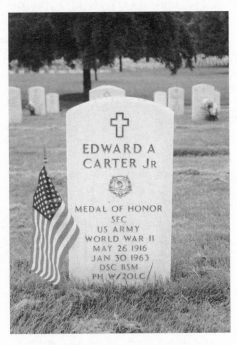

Grave of Edward A. Carter, Jr., USA

awarded the Medal of Honor by President William Clinton in a special ceremony at the White House. Edward Carter's Medal of Honor was presented to his family. Carter's Medal of Honor citation reads as follows:

> For extraordinary heroism on March 23, 1945, as a member of Seventh Army Infantry Company Number 1 (Provisional), 56th Armored Infantry Battalion, 12th Armored Division, near Speyer, Germany. When the tank he was riding received heavy bazooka and small arms fire, Sergeant Carter voluntarily attempted to lead a three man group across an open field. Two of his men were killed and the third seriously wounded. Continuing alone, he was wounded five times and finally was forced to take cover. As eight enemy riflemen attempted to capture him, Sergeant Carter killed six of them and captured the remaining two. He then crossed the field, using as a shield his two prisoners from whom he obtained valuable information concerning the disposition of enemy troops.

On January 14, 1997, the day after President William Clinton awarded Carter's family the Medal of Honor, Edward A. Carter was reinterred in Arlington National Cemetery, Arlington, Virginia.

1st Lieutenant John R. Fox, USA

366th U.S. Infantry

John Robert Fox was born on May 18, 1915. He entered the service on February 28, 1941.

The official story concerning Lieutenant Fox's Medal of Honor is that on December 25, 1944, Lieutenant Fox volunteered to serve as an artillery forward observer in the village of Sommocolonia in the Serchio Valley in Italy. Lieutenant Fox, together with Lieutenant Graham Jenkins and 53 men of the 366th, moved forward and established the forward observation post. Lieutenant Fox chose the second story of a house in the village as his observation post.

On the morning of December 26th, Lieutenant Fox found that the Germans were making an attempt to overrun his position and overwhelm his small command. Lieutenant Fox got on the radio and called down artillery fire just 60 yards from his position. The 598th Field Artillery laid down a barrage at the requested coordinates. At 11:00 A.M., Lieutenant Fox was on the radio again, this time asking for artillery fire right on his own position. Lieutenant Otis Zachary, who took the message, was a friend of Fox and balked at giving the order. The colonel commanding the battalion also balked, calling Fox for confirmation of his request. "There are hundreds of them coming. Put everything you've got on my O.P.!" was the response Fox gave him. The colonel, still unwilling to give the order to fire on his own men, called up the chain of command to division to get approval. The order was given and Lieutenant Zachary gave the order for four guns to walk their fire, converging on his friend's position.

Lieutenant Fox, Lieutenant Jenkins and all their other men were killed during the artillery barrage as were hundreds of the German soldiers attacking the observation post.

The unofficial version is supplied by 2nd Lieutenant Jefferson L. Jordan of the 370th Infantry Regiment, who was assigned to investigate the deaths of Fox and his men. The 366th had been thrown back to Barga in the German counterattack, and it was a week before the Americans were able to recover the ground and the bodies of the men of Fox's command. Lieutenant Jordan's investigation led him to believe that Lieutenant Fox and his men were killed not by the artillery bombardment, but rather that while Fox was attempting to lead his men out of Sommocolonia, he his men were killed by an aerial bombardment by American dive bombers as they attempted to escape the German attack.

The 366th put in the names of both Lieutenant Fox and Lieutenant Jenkins for medals for their conduct, but nothing more was heard about the matter. The men of the 366th were certain there were no medals awarded because the men were black. The paperwork was undoubtedly either lost or destroyed and John Fox was not even awarded the Distinguished Service Cross until 1982.

The Distinguished Service Cross awarded to Lieutenant Fox for his bravery was upgraded to a Medal of Honor on January 13, 1997, after an investigation by the Army as to why no black soldiers had been awarded the Medal of Honor during World War II. Fox's Medal of Honor was presented to his family by President William J. Clinton at a special ceremony at the White House.

Lieutenant Fox's Medal of Honor citation reads as follows:

> For extraordinary heroism on December 26, 1944, while
> serving as a member of Cannon Company, 366th Infantry

Regiment, 92nd Infantry Division, near Sommocolonia, Italy. Being greatly outnumbered, most of the U.S. infantry forces had withdrawn from the town, but Lieutenant Fox and some other members of his observer party voluntarily remained on the second floor of a house to direct defensive artillery fire. After acknowledging the danger, Lieutenant Fox insisted all fire power be directed at him, as this was the only way to defeat the attacking enemy soldiers. Later, when a counter attack retook the position, Lieutenant Fox's riddled body was found along with bodies of approximately one hundred German soldiers.

John Robert Fox is buried at Colebrook Cemetery, Whitman, Massachusetts. He is survived by his widow.

Private First Class
Willy F. James, Jr., USA
413th Infantry

Willy F. James was born on March 18, 1920, at Kansas City, Missouri. He enlisted in the Army on September 11, 1942.

Private Willy F. James earned the Medal of Honor on April 7, 1945, near Lippoldsberg, Germany. His citation reads as follows:

> For extraordinary heroism in action on 7 April 1945 as a member of Company G, 413th Infantry, 104th Division, near Lippoldsberg, Germany. As lead scout during a maneuver to secure and expand a vital bridgehead, Private First Class James was the first to draw enemy fire. He was pinned down for over an hour, during which time he observed enemy positions in detail. Returning to his platoon, he assisted in working out a new plan of maneuver. He then led a squad in the assault, accurately designating targets as he advanced, until he was killed by enemy machine gun fire while going to the aid of his fatally wounded platoon leader. Private First Class James' fearless, self-assigned actions, coupled with his diligent devotion to duty, exemplified the finest traditions of the Armed Forces.

Private Willy F. James was killed in action on April 7, 1945, near Lippoldsberg, Germany. He is buried in the Margraten Cemetery in the Netherlands. He is survived by his widow.

Some of Private James' comrades in arms dispute that he performed the deed of valor for which he was awarded the Medal of Honor. Donald Weishaupt, a former platoon commander with the 413th Infantry, claims that James did not deserve the Distinguished Service Cross let alone a Medal of Honor. "It's a discredit to the people who really won the Medal of Honor." James' Distinguished Service Cross, which was upgraded to a Medal of Honor, was based upon eyewitness testimony by William S. Harden and John D. Helmsley. Both Harden and Helmsley are African Americans. The Shaw Commission, which investigated the incident, confirmed the eyewitness reports and recommended James and nine others for the Medal of Honor. The Army then performed its own investigation and cut the recommendations from ten to seven, and Willy James' name was still on the list.

His belated Medal of Honor was awarded by President William J. Clinton on January 13, 1997, in a special ceremony at the White House.

Staff Sergeant Ruben Rivers, USA
761st Tank Battalion

Ruben Rivers was born on October 30, 1918. He entered the service on January 15, 1942, from Oklahoma City, Oklahoma.

Sergeant Rivers earned the Medal of Honor on November 7, 1944, at a railroad crossing near Guebling, France. Sergeant Rivers was awarded the Silver Star for his actions, but the Army review panel set up in 1988 to investigate why no African Americans had been awarded the Medal of Honor during World War II determined that Rivers should have been awarded the Medal of Honor.

Sergeant Ruben Rivers' Medal of Honor citation reads follows:

> For extraordinary heroism in action during 15–19 November 1944 while serving as a member of Company A, 761st Tank Battalion near Guebling, France. Rivers' tank was hit by a mine while it was advancing. Severely wounded in the leg, he refused treatment and evacuation, took command of another tank, and advanced with his company. Repeatedly refusing evacuation, Sergeant Rivers continued to direct his tank's fire at enemy positions for three days. On the morning of the 19th he opened fire on the enemy tanks, covering Company A as they withdrew. While doing so, Rivers' tank was hit by enemy fire, which killed him and wounded the others crew members.

On November 16, 1944, Sergeant Rivers' Sherman Tank hit a land mine at a railroad crossing outside of Guebling, France. Rivers' right leg was laid open to the bone above the knee. Sergeant Rivers refused a morphine injection as well as medical evacuation, instead taking command of another tank at the head of the column. Sergeant Rivers fought on, with his badly wounded leg bound in heavy bandages, refusing evacuation even when urged to by his commanding officer, Captain David Williams. "You need me," was Sergeant Rivers' reply.

Three days later on November 19, Rivers' battalion was attacking towards the town of Bourgaltroff when its lead tank was hit by 88-mm antitank fire. When Sergeant Rivers was ordered to pull back, he radioed his commanding officer that he had spotted the enemy positions stating: "I see 'em; we'll fight 'em." Sergeant River took his tank forward and engaged the Germans. Rivers was killed when a shell his tank turret. He gallantly gave his life for his country.

Ruben Rivers is buried in the American Battle Monument Cemetery in France. He was survived by nine brothers and sisters.

In 1988 critics of the Army charged that the reason no blacks had received the Medal of Honor during either World War I or World War II was simply a case of racial prejudice. Sensitive to the accusations, the Army commissioned a review of all award recommendations made for blacks during this period. The investigation demonstrated without question that African American soldiers in both World War I and World War II had indeed performed deeds of valor deserving of the Medal of Honor.

Sergeant Ruben Rivers was one of the ten African Americans cited by the investigation as deserving of the Medal of Honor. After receiving the commission's report, the Army performed its own investigation and the number of candidates was cut from ten to eight. On January 13, 1997, President William Clinton presented Sergeant Rivers' Medal of Honor to his family.

1st Lieutenant Charles L. Thomas, USA

614th Tank Destroyer Battalion

Charles L. Thomas was born on April 17, 1920, in Birmingham, Alabama. Thomas was raised in Detroit, Michigan, attending Cass

Technical High School and Wayne University before being drafted into the Army on January 20, 1942.

Thomas completed his basic training at Camp Wolters, Texas, and was part of a cadre sent to Camp Carson to become officers for the 614th Tank Destroyer Battalion. On March 11, 1943, Thomas was commissioned as a 1st Lieutenant, and assigned as the commanding officer of Company C, 614th Tank Destroyer Battalion, 103rd Infantry Division.

Lieutenant Thomas earned the Medal of Honor on December 14, 1944, in an assault on German positions near Climbach, France, just five miles from the German border. Lieutenant Thomas volunteered to lead his platoon into a valley, which he knew could only be approached by one road but was covered by German artillery. Lieutenant Thomas assigned himself the point position in his company's assault on the German positions. Thomas would later explain that he had volunteered his platoon because "I knew that if the job could be done these men could do it because they could and would fight; they were proud and they were good. Training and discipline were the key and they had plenty of both."

Leading the attack in an armored M20 Scout Car, Lieutenant Thomas intended to draw the enemy's artillery fire and therefore locate their positions for his company. The Germans held their fire until Thomas' platoon was well advanced into the valley and then opened up with mortar and artillery fire. The Germans quickly got their range and one shell blew out the scout car's windshield, showering Lieutenant Thomas with glass and shrapnel. The next round blew the wheels of the scout car. As the survivors of his platoon scrambled for cover, the wounded Lieutenant Thomas climbed on top of the vehicle, and opened fire on the German infantry with a .50 caliber machine-gun. A conspicuous target, the indomitable Lieutenant Thomas was hit several more times in his arms, chest, stomach and legs, but continued in his exposed position, firing his machine gun to defend his comrades.

Thomas then crawled under the scout car and from that position directed the positioning of his men and directed their fire of their anti-tank guns upon the enemy. By this time Lieutenant Thomas was a mess to behold, although he kept giving orders and urging his men to do their best. A one-sided artillery duel had begun and unless Thomas could get his guns deployed and firing, all the men were going to be killed and he knew it. Thomas later said that during this time, he hung on to one thought, "Deploy the guns and start firing or we are dead."

Thomas' men, seeing him badly wounded and still performing his duty, were pushed to even greater effort. They responded to their leader's orders. "My men," Thomas would say later, "were a fine disciplined bunch and their deployment on my orders was as normal as breathing even under the heated circumstances. Normally the one who gets off the first shot is the victor. We did not have this advantage but their speed and accuracy made up the difference."

Lieutenant Thomas refused to be evacuated until he had seen that the men in his platoon were well positioned and their guns deployed and firing. Even then, Thomas refused evacuation until an officer who had commanded a company was present to relieve him. For as Lieutenant Thomas explained, "This was hardly the place to learn."

Thomas also said, "I was conscious the whole time and in command until the officer arrived to relieve me. My men were getting their guns into position with the whole world erupting around them. They were doing it swiftly and in good fashion in spite of the casualties we were beginning to sustain. In just a few minutes we were returning the fire. They were functioning to a lesser degree, just as I was, automatically. I knew what had to be done. That is why I would not leave or should I say allow myself to be evacuated until the officer to replace me was on hand and all our guns were firing."

Lieutenant Thomas was awarded the Distinguished Service Cross for his gallantry. Still recuperating from his wounds, Lieutenant Thomas returned to Detroit, Michigan, in March 1945 to a hero's welcome. One Detroit paper wrote: "German shells took the wheels off his armored car, but it took more than that to stop Captain Charles L. Thomas and 34 other black infantrymen who fought their way through artillery, mortar and machine-gun fire to pierce the Siegfried Line and win a position on German soil."

The modest Thomas played down his own heroics, telling one reporter, "I was sent to locate and draw enemy fire, but I didn't mean to draw that much."

In the years that followed, Charles L. Thomas became one of America's forgotten heroes. Charles L. Thomas died of cancer on February 15, 1980. At the time of his death, the local papers did not even print his obituary. He was buried in the West Lawn Cemetery, in Wayne, Michigan.

This situation was rectified in part after an investigation commissioned by the Secretary of the Army in 1993 determined that Thomas should have been awarded the Medal of Honor for his valor. On January 13, 1997, Thomas was one of the seven African Americans belatedly honored by their country for heroism that was "above and beyond the call of duty." President William Clinton awarded the Medal of Honor to Sandra Johnson, Thomas' niece, at a special ceremony at the White House.

First Lieutenant Charles L. Thomas' Medal of Honor citation reads as follows:

> For extraordinary heroism on December 14, 1944, while serving in Company C, 614th Tank Destroyer Battalion (Towed), 103rd Infantry Division near Climbach, France. His armored scout car was subjected to intense enemy artillery, self-propelled gun, and small arms fire. Wounded by the initial burst of hostile fire, Lieutenant Thomas signaled the remainder of the column to halt and despite the severity of his wounds, assisted his crew-members in obtaining cover. Upon leaving the scant protection the vehicle afforded, Lieutenant Thomas was again subjected to a hail of enemy fire, which inflicted multiple gunshot wounds in his chest, legs and left arm. Despite the pain he ordered and directed the disposition and emplacement of two anti-tank guns, which effectively returned the enemy's fire. He refused to be evacuated until he was certain a junior officer was in full control of the situation.

Private George Watson, USA

29th Quartermaster Regiment

George Watson was born on March 14, 1914, at Birmingham, Alabama. He enlisted in the Army on September 11, 1942, and was assigned to the 29th Quartermaster Regiment which was serving in the Pacific Theater.

On March 8, 1943, Private Watson was aboard the Dutch steamer *Jacob* near Porloch Harbor, when the ship was attacked by Japanese bombers. The ship was all but defenseless against its airborne enemies. Bombs exploded in the water all around the steamer causing massive fountains of water to go shooting into the air. It is hard to be a target with no chance to strike back. Bombs hit the *Jacob*, tearing metal and sending iron shrapnel everywhere. The *Jacob* took a pounding before the bombers finally left the ship burning and sinking.

The ship's captain gave the order to abandon ship, and soldiers and sailors jumped into the sea. The few life rafts available were inflated and everyone who could swam for the rafts and struggled to get aboard. George Watson swam for the raft too but not before he grabbed a soldier who could not swim and pulled him along. At the raft, Watson assisted the soldier aboard but made no effort to get in the raft himself. Ignoring his own safety, the courageous solder went after another man who could not swim and then another and another.

Again and again Watson would find a man struggling in the water and swim with him for a raft. The *Jacob* was getting low in the water. To stay in the ocean now anywhere in the vicinity of the stricken ship was a great danger. When the ship went under it would created a vacuum which would suck everything in the area under the water. Watson knew of the danger, but there were still men floundering in the water and he could not take for himself the safety of the raft and just leave them to die. While swimming out to rescue another of his comrades, the *Jacob* sank below the surface. Weakened by his exertions, he was dragged down by the suction of the sinking ship and was drowned. Private Watson's valorous actions earned for him the Medal of Honor.

Private George Watson's citation reads as follows:

> For extraordinary heroism in action on 8 March 1943. Private Watson was on board a ship which was attacked and hit by enemy bombers. When the ship was abandoned, Private Watson, instead of seeking to save himself, remained in the water assisting several soldiers who could not swim to reach the safety of the raft. This heroic action, which subsequently cost him his life, resulted in the saving of several of his comrades. Weakened by his exertions, he was dragged down by the suction of the sinking ship and was drowned. Private Watson's extraordinarily valorous actions, daring leadership, and self-sacrificing devotion to his fellow-man exemplify the finest traditions of military service.

George Watson's body was never recovered. His name is inscribed on the wall-of-the-missing at the Manila American Battle Monument Cemetery in the Philippines.

On January 13, 1997, George Watson was one of the seven African Americans belatedly honored by their country for heroism that was, "above and beyond the call of duty." Since Private George Watson has no known living relatives, President William Clinton awarded Watson's Medal of Honor to sergeant major of the Army, Eugene McKinney, at a special ceremony at the White House. Sergeant Major McKinney also happens to be an African American.

Chapter 7

The Korean War (1950–1953)

On June 25, 1950, North Korean troops invaded South Korea, attacking across the 38th parallel. By June 30th, the first U.S. ground troops had entered the conflict as part of the United Nations force committed to pushing the North Koreans back across the 38th parallel. When the Korean War broke out, the Army was still rigidly segregated and racist.

The all black 24th and 25th U.S. Infantry Regiments, which could trace their history back to 1866 when Congress first authorized the creation of six African American regiments for service in the regular U.S. Army, were sent to Korea. In Korea, however, the 24th Infantry generally performed poorly in the fighting. This fact was seized upon by those in the military who already had a prejudice against black soldiers and again led to the stereotyping of all African Americans as unreliable soldiers.

Strong forces were at work, however, which sought to make the military an integrated organization where merit, not race, would be the measure of a man's worth. On October 1, 1951, against strong opposition, President Harry Truman, as commander-in-chief of the U.S. armed forces, ordered the integration of all of U.S. armed forces beginning with those engaged with the enemy in Korea.

In implementing the president's order, the 24th Infantry was dissolved and the black soldiers from the 24th were distributed throughout other regiments in Korea.

Two African American soldiers earned the Medal of Honor in Korea. Interestingly, both men were from the disreputable 24th U.S. Infantry and earned their medals before the regiment was disbanded.

Sergeant Cornelius H. Charlton, USA

24th U.S. Infantry

Cornelius H. Charlton was born on July 24, 1929, at East Gulf, Raleigh County, West Virginia. He was the eighth of 17 children in his family. He was also the largest, weighing 15 pounds at birth. When Cornelius, who was nicknamed "Connie," was 15 years old his father, who had been a coal miner for 38 years, moved his family to the Bronx, New York, where he took a job as an apartment building superintendent. Charlton attended James Madison High School. He expressed a strong desire to join the Army but his parents would not cosign his enlistment papers until he obtained his high school diploma. In November 1946, Charlton graduated from high school and enlisted in the U.S. Army.

After basic training Charlton was sent to Germany for occupation duty. He finished his first enlistment there. After reenlisting Charlton was assigned to the Aberdeen Proving Grounds in Maryland. In early 1950, Charlton, now a sergeant, was transferred to Okinawa.

When the Eighth Army broke out of the Pusan Perimeter, Charlton's unit was sent from Okinawa to Korea. Sergeant Charlton, however, was kept behind the lines, assigned primarily to administrative tasks. Charlton grew restless at his job. It was not his style to sit behind the lines doing paperwork while other men were fighting and dying. Sergeant Charlton finally requested his C.O. to a transfer to a combat unit. The C.O. reluctantly agreed to Charlton's request. "I hope you know what you are doing Sergeant," the captain said. "You can get killed up there."

"I just don't feel right sitting back here while others are doing the fighting up north," was Charlton's simple response. With the stroke of a pen he got his wish and was transferred to Company C, 24th Infantry Regiment, 25th Infantry Division, and was on his way north to the combat zone.

The 24th Infantry was an all black unit, which had not yet been integrated. At the time that Sergeant Charlton arrived, its morale had hit rock bottom. The regiment had a reputation of bugging out in the face of the enemy. So pervasive was its reputation that the black GIs had adopted the self-deprecating song "Bug-out Blues" as their unofficial regimental song.

Company C's commander, Captain Gordon E. Gullikson, was suspicious of Sergeant Charlton. Anyone who would leave a safe cushy job in the rear and come to the front lines needed to be watched carefully. What Gullikson saw, however, pleased him greatly. Sergeant Charlton turned his squad into a first class fighting outfit. Whenever they had spare time, Charlton drilled his men. As they trained their skills got better and their self-confidence grew. Morale in Charlton's unit started to increase. Two months after his arrival in Company C, Captain Gullikson had promoted Charlton over several senior NCOs to be platoon sergeant of the third platoon and had recommended Charlton for a battlefield commission.

The lieutenant's bars would have to wait, however, until after Operation Piledriver was complete. The first day of Operation Piledriver, Charlton's battalion was held in reserve. The Third Battalion took its first objective, Hill 1147, without much trouble. But the second objective, Hill 543, was a much harder nut to crack. Attack after attack of the Third Battalion was bloodily repulsed by the stubborn Chinese defenders. After spending a miserable rainy night on the base of Hill 543, the Third Battalion attacked again but was once more repulsed. At noon, Charlton's battalion got word that it would replace the Third battalion and take over the assault. Charlton's platoon would lead the way.

A devastating air strike rocked the bolder-strewn hill with high explosives and napalm bombs. As the last plane dropped its load, Company C started its

Sergeant Cornelius H. Charlton, USA

assault. Halfway up, the hill erupted into flames as the Chinese showered the Americans with artillery and mortar fire. Shrapnel struck men
down all along the line. The platoon leader, in command for just two
weeks, was severely wounded in the inferno. Before the leaderless men
could become disorganized, Charlton stepped into the breach, rallied
his men and led them up the hill.

The assault stalled as the black soldiers came under an intense hail
of machine-gun fire. Most of the platoon dived for cover, but not Charlton. With his gun blazing, Charlton charged up the hill. With grenades
and rife fire he destroyed two Chinese positions, killing six enemy
defenders.

With his position temporarily secured, Charlton rallied his men.
The training was paying of, the men of the platoon were somewhat
shaken, but their fighting spirit was still intact and they were ready to
follow where Sergeant Charlton would lead. Charlton sent the wounded
to the rear and moved out with the 20 able-bodied men that were left.
As the platoon's renewed push neared the crest of the hill, concussion
and fragment grenades poured down on the men from the defenders on
the crest.

Sergeant Charlton felt several grenades kick past him, but then was
thrown to the ground by an explosion. Blood poured from a large hole
in his chest. Charlton was momentarily stunned but regained his wits
and shrugged off the medic who was trying to treat his wounds. There
was a job to do and Charlton was going to do it. His men needed his
leadership and he was not going to be evacuated. Charlton lay there for
a period of time studying the hill and formulating his plan.

The sergeant called out instructions to his men and on his signal
they again attempted to rush the summit. Although severely wounded,
Charlton must have been proud of the performance of his men. Fewer
than 20 were left but they were fighting. Black soldiers, using the skills
he had trained into them, were fighting the way he knew they could. He
was not going to let them down. The new assault was again met with a
barrage of grenades and more casualties were taken.

The casualties were sent to the rear and Charlton and his men prepared to make the final rush. He was down to just a dozen men but they
were going to take this hill. Sergeant Charlton's indomitable spirit,
courage and personal strength became an inspiration to his men. Shout-
ing "Let's go! C'mon! Let's go!" Sergeant Charlton led the final charge
up the hill. Braving an intense enemy fire, Sergeant Charlton and not
more than eight of his men drove the Chinese off the summit of Hill 543.

With the summit now under his control, Sergeant Charlton could see that the Chinese position on the reverse slope would have to be neutralized in order to hold the ground he had taken at such a great cost. Sergeant Charlton flattened himself on a rock and observed the Chinese position. There appeared to be no way to assault the position except by a direct frontal assault. Yelling to his men, "Cover me!" he jumped to his feet and charged down the hill, firing his own rifle as fast as he could.

A grenade knocked Charlton down again and when he struggled back onto his feet he was bleeding from a dozen new wounds. But Sergeant Charlton kept on moving down the hill, firing his rifle. At last the position fell silent, the last Chinese having been killed. Sergeant Charlton collapsed in front of the position he had single-handedly attacked. Medics rushed to his side trying to save his life but there was nothing they could do. The courageous Sergeant Charlton died in Korea on the top of Hill 543.

Charlton's men, enraged at the death of their leader, cleared the remainder of the Chinese from the hill, taking one fortified position after another.

Sergeant Charlton's Medal of Honor citation reads as follows:

> Sergeant Charlton, a member of Company C, distinguished himself by conspicuous gallantry and intrepidity above and beyond the call of duty in action against the enemy. His platoon was attacking heavily defended hostile positions on commanding ground when the leader was wounded and evacuated. Sergeant Charlton assumed command, rallied the men, and spearheaded the assault against the hill. Personally eliminating 2 hostile positions and killing 6 of the enemy with his rifle fire and grenades, he continued up the slope until the unit suffered heavy casualties and became pinned down. Regrouping the men he led them forward only to be again hurled back by a shower of grenades. Despite a severe chest wound, Sergeant Charlton refused medical attention and led a third daring charge, which carried to the crest of the ridge. Observing that the remaining emplacement, which had retarded the advance was situated on the reverse slope, he charged it alone, was again hit by a grenade but raked the position with a devastating fire which eliminated it and routed the defenders. The wounds received during his daring exploits resulted in his death but his indomitable courage, superb leadership, and gallant self-sacrifice reflect the highest credit upon himself, the infantry, and the military service.

Sergeant Cornelius H. Charlton was killed in action at Chipo-ri, Korea, on June 2, 1951. Charlton's Medal of Honor was presented to his parents, Van and Esther Charlton, on March 12, 1952, at the Pentagon, by Frank C. Pace, the Secretary of the Army. Cornelius H. Charlton is buried at the American Legion Cemetery, at Beckly, West Virginia.

Private First Class
William H. Thompson, USA

24th U.S. Infantry

William Henry Thompson had a hard life. He was born out of wedlock on August 16, 1927, in Brooklyn, New York. Thompson dropped out of school at an early age. Most of his teen years were spent on the streets of New York. Thompson entered the service in October 1945 at Bronx County, New York. His first two-year tour of duty was spent in Adak, Alaska.

Thompson fit in well in the regular Army. He appeared to have found a home. He was quiet and hard working. His uniform and machine gun were always kept spotless and he was one of the best marksmen in the regiment. He reenlisted in 1948 and was assigned to the 6th Infantry Division, then on occupation duty in Korea. When the 6th transferred back to the States Thompson was transferred to the 24th Infantry Regiment then stationed in Japan.

Private Thompson earned the Medal of Honor on August 6, 1950, near Haman, Korea. A platoon from Company M, the heavy weapons unit of the 24th Regiment, had just completed supporting a rifle company in clearing one of the hamlets of Haman. They had fallen back to an assembly area when they were attacked by units of the North Korean Army. Enemy automatic weapons fire raked through the Americans. Many of the men panicked and fled into the night. Those that did not flee were organized into a tight defense by 2nd Lieutenant Herbert H. Wilson.

Lieutenant Wilson ordered the two machine guns of Company M into action. No sooner had the guns opened fire than one of them was knocked out of action by an exploding grenade. Now Private Thompson's machine gun was the only automatic weapon answering the North

Korean's fire. The enemy's fire and grenade attacks focused on his position, but Private Thompson calmly continued sending out bursts of fire at the enemy.

When the NKA soldiers renewed their attack, Private Thompson took a position directly in their path. His actions spoke louder than words in the language that every soldier understands: "To get to my buddies your going to have to get by me and that will be over my dead body." All around his machine gun NKA soldiers were mowed down by his deadly accurate fire. Belt after belt of .30 caliber ammo disappeared

William Thompson, USA

into Thompson's machine gun and the NKA were driven to cover.

In the lull Lieutenant Wilson ordered his men to fall back to higher ground. When Private Thompson did not respond to the order Lieutenant Wilson crawled out to his position. He found that Thompson had been hit several times and was bleeding heavily. "Let's go," Wilson said "We can get out of here now." But Thompson refused. He told the lieutenant that he knew he was dying and that he planned to stay where he was. Even during their conversation, Private Thompson continued to fire short bursts from his gun at any NKA soldier foolish enough to show his head.

Lieutenant Wilson now ordered Thompson to withdraw but again he refused. "I may not get out," he told the lieutenant, "but I'll take a lot of them with me." Wilson called for two non-commissioned officers to drag Thompson off his gun. They tried but the wounded Thompson broke away. The NKA were up renewing their assault. "Get out of here!" Thompson screamed. "I'll cover you." Then he returned to delivering his deadly fire on those that had attacked his men, those who had all but killed him. But he was not dead yet.

With the sound of Thompson's machine gun ringing in their ears, Lieutenant Wilson and his men withdrew to higher ground where they could organize a better defense. Behind them Thompson's machine gun chattered away. Explosions rang out into the night. Then Thompson's machine gun fell silent.

A few days later when Company M retook the area, they found Thompson's lifeless body. Scattered all around him was the evidence that he had kept his word. He had taken a lot of them with him.

William Thompson's Medal of Honor citation reads as follows:

> Private First Class Thompson distinguished himself by conspicuous gallantry and intrepidity above and beyond the call of duty in action against the enemy. While his platoon was reorganizing under cover of darkness, fanatical enemy forces in overwhelming strength launched a surprise attack on the unit. Private First Class Thompson set up his machine gun in the path of the onslaught and swept the enemy with withering fire, pinning them down momentarily, thus permitting the remainder of his platoon to withdraw to a more tenable position. Although hit repeatedly by grenade fragments and small-arms fire, he resisted all efforts of his comrades to induce him to withdraw, steadfastly remained at his machine gun and continued to deliver deadly, accurate fire until mortally wounded by an enemy grenade. Private First Class Thompson's dauntless courage and gallant self-sacrifice reflect the highest credit on himself and uphold the esteemed traditions of military service.

Private William Henry Thompson was killed in action on August 6, 1950, at Haman, Korea. General Omar N. Bradley presented Thompson's Medal of Honor to his mother on June 21, 1951, at a special ceremony at the Pentagon. Thompson is buried at the Long Island National Cemetery at Farmingdale, New York.

Chapter 8

The Vietnam War (1960–1975)

Between 1960 and 1975, several hundred thousand African Americans served in the U.S. Army, Navy and Marine Corps in Vietnam. Black soldiers played a major role in all of the war's many bitter battles and skirmishes. Many awards were earned by black soldiers during the Vietnam War, including 20 Medals of Honor.

The Vietnam War was the first conflict in which it was not necessary for African Americans to again prove their combat capabilities. Optimism about the future of black personnel in the military service can justifiably be based upon the numerous achievements of black soldiers in the Vietnam War.

Far from keeping black soldiers, sailors and marines out of combat, in Vietnam perhaps the opposite problem existed. During the buildup of American strength in Vietnam, the Selective Service System inducted as many as 60 percent of the eligible blacks while only drafting 30 percent of the eligible whites. The liberal granting of educational deferments, which were disproportionately given to whites, caused this inequity. Upon entering the service, educational disadvantages resulting from second rate schools tended to steer black soldiers and marines into combat roles. These facts led to the perception among many that Vietnam was a rich man's war but a poor man's fight, with blacks doing a disproportionate share of the fighting.

Racism had not been totally abolished in the military. When Dr. Martin Luther King was murdered, white sailors at Cua Viet donned makeshift white robes and paraded around in imitation of the Ku Klux Klan. At the same time, Confederate battle flags were unfurled over Cam Ranh Bay and Da Nang. The racism, while serious, was not institutionalized. Efforts were made at the highest levels in both the Army and the Navy to make the military services as race neutral as possible.

In Vietnam African American soldiers, sailors and marines again proudly served their country. Many of them sacrificed their lives for the dream of freedom and equality, which they did not yet fully enjoy at home. Fifteen African American soldiers and five African American marines earned the Medal of Honor in Vietnam. Their stories follow.

Private First Class
James Anderson, Jr., USMC

3rd U.S. Marines

James Anderson, Jr., was born on January 22, 1947, at Los Angeles, Los Angeles County, California. Anderson enlisted in the Marine Corps at Los Angeles, California, and was assigned to 2d Platoon, Company F, 2d Battalion, 3d Marines, 3d Marine Division.

On February 28, 1967, Private James Anderson, Jr., became the first black marine to earn the Medal of Honor, when he covered an exploding grenade with his body to save the lives of his comrades. His citation reads as follows:

> For conspicuous gallantry and intrepidity at the risk of his life above and beyond the call of duty. Company F was advancing in dense jungle northwest of Cam Lo in an effort to extract a heavily besieged reconnaissance patrol. Private First Class Anderson's platoon was the lead element and had advanced only about 200 meters when they were brought under extremely intense enemy small-arms and automatic weapons fire. The platoon reacted swiftly, getting on line as best they could in the thick terrain, and began returning fire. Private First Class Anderson found himself tightly bunched together with the other members of the platoon only 20 meters from the enemy positions. As the fire fight continued several of the men were wounded by the deadly enemy assault. Suddenly, an enemy grenade landed in the midst

of the marines and rolled alongside Private First Class Anderson's head. Unhesitatingly and with complete disregard for his personal safety, he reached out, grasped the grenade, pulled it to his chest and curled around it as it went off. Although several marines received shrapnel from the grenade, his body absorbed the major force of the explosion. In this singularly heroic act, Private First Class Anderson saved his comrades from serious injury and possible death. His personal heroism, extraordinary valor, and inspirational supreme self-sacrifice reflected great credit upon himself and the Marine Corps and upheld the highest traditions of the U.S. Naval Service. He gallantly gave his life for his country.

Private James Anderson, Jr., was killed in action on February 28, 1967, in the Republic of Vietnam. In recognition of his extraordinary courage, which saved the lives of several of his fellow Marines, Secretary of the Navy Paul R. Ignatius presented the Medal of Honor to Anderson's family on August 21, 1968, at a special ceremony at the Marine Barracks, Washington, D.C.

Sergeant Webster Anderson, USA

101st U.S. Airborne Infantry

Webster Anderson was born on July 15, 1933, at Winnsboro, Fairfield County, South Carolina, the son of Frizell Anderson. Anderson enlisted in the Army on September 11, 1953, at Winnsboro, and was assigned to Battery A, 2d Battalion, 320th Field Artillery, 101st Airborne Infantry Division (Airmobile). Anderson served at Camp Chaffie, Arkansas; Fort Bragg, North Carolina; Fort Campbell, Kentucky; the Dominican Republic; Vietnam, and Fort Gordon, Georgia.

In the spring of 1967 Sergeant Anderson was serving with the elite 1st Brigade of the 101st Airborne Division, which had been assigned as a part of operation Task Force Oregon. Task Force Oregon was composed of three Army Brigades, which were operating in the VC-dominated province of Quang Ngai.

Throughout the spring and summer the 101st Airborne played a game of hide and seek with the 2nd VC Regiment, which was the primary opposition in the province. The VC tended to avoid battle with the Americans unless they could bring substantially superior numbers to bear. On October 15, 1967, the VC were able to obtain the mismatch that they were seeking and launched a ferocious attack against Battery A, 2nd Battalion, 320th Artillery, at its fire support base near the coastal city of Tam Ky. The goal of the VC was to destroy the fire base and retreat into the jungle before the Americans could bring up reinforcements. It as at this battle Sergeant Anderson earned the Medal of Honor. His citation reads as follows:

> Sergeant First Class Anderson distinguished himself by conspicuous gallantry and intrepidity in action while serving as chief of section in Battery A, against a hostile force. During the early morning hours Battery A's defensive position was attacked by a determined North Vietnamese Army infantry unit supported by heavy mortar, recoilless rifle, rocket propelled grenade and automatic weapon fire. The initial enemy onslaught breached the battery defensive perimeter. Sergeant First Class Anderson, with complete disregard for his personal safety, mounted the exposed parapet of his howitzer position and became the mainstay of the defense of the battery position. Sergeant First Class Anderson directed devastating direct howitzer fire on the assaulting enemy while providing rifle and grenade defensive fire against enemy soldiers attempting to overrun his gun section position. While protecting his crew and directing their fire against the enemy from his exposed position, 2 enemy grenades exploded at his feet knocking him down and severely wounding him in the legs. Despite the excruciating pain and though not able to stand, Sergeant First Class Anderson valorously propped himself on the parapet and continued to direct howitzer fire upon the closing enemy and to encourage his men to fight on. Seeing an enemy grenade land within the gun pit near a wounded member of his gun crew, Sergeant First Class Anderson, heedless of his own safety, seized the grenade and attempted to throw it over the parapet to save his men. As the grenade was thrown from the position it exploded and Sergeant First Class Anderson was again grievously wounded. Although only partially conscious and severely wounded, Sergeant First Class Anderson refused medical evacuation and continued to encourage his men in the defense of the position. Sergeant First Class Anderson, by his inspirational leadership, professionalism, devotion to duty and complete disregard for his welfare, was able to maintain the defense of his section position and to defeat a determined attack. Sergeant First Class Anderson's gallantry and extraordinary heroism at the risk of his life above and beyond the call of duty are in the highest traditions of the military service and reflect great credit upon himself, his unit, and the U.S. Army.

As a result of the battle Sergeant Anderson lost both of his legs. It took the gutsy Anderson nearly a year to recuperate from his wounds. On November 29, 1969, Sergeant Anderson stood proudly on two artificial legs as President Richard M. Nixon presented to him the Medal of Honor at a special ceremony at the White House.

In addition to the Medal of Honor, Sergeant Anderson also earned the Purple Heart, three Good Conduct Medals, National Defense Service Medal, Vietnam Service Medal, Master Parachutist Badge, and the Vietnam Campaign Medal (Vietnamese).

Sergeant Eugene Ashley, Jr., USA

5th U.S. Special Forces Group (Airborne), 1st Special Forces

Eugene Ashley, Jr., was born on October 12, 1931, in Wilmington, New Hanover County, North Carolina. Ashley attended Alexander Hamilton High School in Brooklyn, New York, before enlisting in the Army on December 5, 1971, at New York City, New York. He received special forces training at Fort Bragg, North Carolina, and was assigned to Company C, 5th Special Forces Group (Airborne), 1st Special Forces.

During his military career, Sergeant Ashley was stationed at Fort Bragg, Germany; South Korea; Okinawa; the Dominican Republic; and Vietnam. Eugene Ashley was married, and he and his wife Barbara had five children.

Sergeant Ashley earned the Medal of Honor on February 6–7, 1968, near Lang Vei, Republic of Vietnam. Lang Vei was a special forces camp just a few miles southwest of Khe Sanh. More than thirty thousand heavily armed North Vietnamese soldiers had surrounded Khe Sanh and the Americans had hunkered down for an attack. The attack never came. The North Vietnamese did, however, attack and overrun the small base at Lang Vei.

The attack on Lang Vei was the first time in the war the North Vietnamese used tanks. With the armor the NVA was able to push most of the Americans and their Vietnamese allies, the Civilian Irregular Defense Group (CIDG), out of the camp. A group of Americans were cut off and surrounded in what was left of Lang Vei. Sergeant Ashley, unwilling to leave his comrades to the NVA, rallied a group of CIDG survivors and launched a counter-attack to free the trapped men. The attack was repulsed. Four more times Sergeant Ashley rallied his men and led them back against the NVA. The fifth attack carried the hill but Sergeant Ashley was severely wounded by machine gun fire while leading his men forward. Sergeant Ashley passed out from loss of blood. He was killed while being carried to the rear by an exploding artillery shell. With the death of Sergeant Ashley the attack dissolved and the survivors fell back on Khe Sanh. Sergeant Ashley's Medal of Honor citation reads as follows:

> Sergeant First Class Ashley distinguished himself by conspicuous gallantry and intrepidity while serving with Detachment A-101, Company C. Sergeant First Class Ashley was the senior special forces advisor of a hastily organized assault force whose mission was to rescue entrapped U.S. special forces advisors at Camp Lang Vei. During the initial attack on the special forces camp by North Vietnamese army forces, Sergeant First Class Ashley supported the camp with high explosive and illumination mortar rounds. When communications were lost with the main camp, he assumed the additional responsibility of directing air strikes and artillery support. Sergeant First Class Ashley organized and equipped a small assault force composed of local friendly personnel. During the ensuing battle, Sergeant First Class Ashley led a total of 5 vigorous assaults against the enemy, continuously exposing himself to a voluminous hail of enemy grenades, machine-gun and automatic weapons fire. Throughout these assaults, he was plagued by numerous booby-trapped satchel charges in all bunkers on his venue of approach. During his fifth and final assault, he adjusted air strikes nearly on top of his assault element, forcing the enemy to withdraw and resulting in friendly control of the summit of the hill. While exposing himself to intense enemy fire, he was seriously wounded by machine-gun fire but continued his mission without regard for his personal safety. After the fifth assault he lost consciousness and was carried from the summit by his comrades only to suffer a fatal wound when an enemy artillery round landed in the area. Sergeant First Class Ashley displayed extraordinary heroism in risking his life in an attempt to save the lives of his entrapped comrades and commanding officer. His total disregard for his personal safety while exposed to enemy observation and automatic weapons fire was an inspiration to all men committed to the assault. The resolute valor with which he led 5 gallant charges placed critical diversionary pressure on the attacking enemy and his valiant efforts carved a channel in the overpowering enemy forces and weapons positions through which the survivors of Camp Lang Vei eventually escaped to freedom. Sergeant First

Class Ashley's bravery at the cost of his life was in the highest traditions of the military service, and reflects great credit upon himself, his unit, and the U.S. Army.

Eugene Ashley, Jr., was killed in action on February 7, 1986, near Lang Vei, Republic of Vietnam. Vice-President Spiro T. Agnew presented Ashley's Medal of Honor to his family on December 2, 1969, at a special presentation at the White House. Eugene Ashley, Jr., is buried at the Rockfish Memorial Cemetery in Fayetteville, North Carolina.

In addition his Medal of Honor, Sergeant Ashley also earned the Bronze Star, the Purple Heart, Good Conduct Medal, Army of Occupation Medal, Korean Service Medal, Armed Forces Expeditionary Medal (Dominican Republic) Vietnam Service Medal, Combat Infantry Badge, Master Parachutist Badge and Vietnam Campaign Medal (Vietnamese).

Private First Class
Oscar P. Austin, USMC

7th U.S. Marines

Oscar Palmer Austin was born on January 15, 1948, at Nacogdoches, Nacogdoches County, Texas, the son of Frank and Mildred Austin. Austin attended Union High School in Phoenix, Arizona, before he was inducted into in the Marine Corps on April 22, 1968, at Phoenix, Arizona. Private Austin completed his basic training at the Marine Corps Recruit Depot in San Diego, California, and was assigned as a munitions specialist to Company E, 2d Battalion, 7th Marines, 1st Marine Division (Rein), FMF.

Private Austin earned the Medal of Honor on February 23, 1969, west of Da Nang, Republic of Vietnam. His citation reads as follows:

> For conspicuous gallantry and intrepidity at the risk of his life above and beyond he call of duty while serving as an assistant machine gunner with Company E, in connection with operations against enemy forces. During the early morning hours Private First Class Austin's observation post was subjected to a fierce ground attack by a large North Vietnamese Army force supported by a heavy volume of hand grenades, satchel charges, and small arms fire. Observing that one of

his wounded companions had fallen unconscious in a position dangerously exposed to the hostile fire, Private First Class
Austin unhesitatingly left the relative security of his fighting
hole and, with complete disregard for his safety, raced across
the fire-swept terrain to assist the marine to a covered loca-
tion. As he neared the casualty, he observed an enemy grenade
land nearby and, reacting instantly, leaped between the
injured marine and the lethal object, absorbing the effects of
its detonation. As he ignored his painful injuries and turned
to examine the wounded man, he saw a North Vietnamese
Army soldier aiming a weapon at his unconscious compan-
ion. With full knowledge of the probable consequences and
thinking only to protect the marine, Private First Class Austin
resolutely threw himself between the casualty and the hostile soldier, and, in so doing, was mortally wounded. Private
First Class Austin's indomitable courage, inspiring initiative
and selfless devotion to duty, upheld the highest traditions of
the Marine Corps and the U.S. Naval Service. He gallantly
gave his life for his country.

Private Oscar Palmer Austin was killed in action, attempting to
save the live of a fellow Marine, on February 23, 1969, west of Da Nang,
Republic of Vietnam. In recognition of his courage, Vice-President Spiro
T. Agnew presented the Medal of Honor to Austin's family on April 20,
1970, at a special ceremony at the White House. Austin is buried in
Greenwood Memorial Cemetery, Phoenix, Arizona.

In addition to the Medal of Honor, Private Austin also earned the
Purple Heart; National Defense Medal; Vietnam Service Medal with two
Bronze Stars and the Vietnam Campaign Medal (Vietnamese).

Sergeant William Maud Bryant, USA

5th U.S. Special Forces

William Maud Bryant was born on February 16, 1933, at Cochran,
Bleckley County, Georgia, the son of Mr. and Mrs. Sebron Bryant.
Bryant's parents divorced when he was young, and he was sent to live
with an uncle in Detroit, Michigan. He completed high school at Newark
Vocational and Technical High School in Newark, New Jersey, before he
joined the Army on March 16, 1953, at Detroit, Michigan.

During his military career, Sergeant Bryant attended various military schools, including basic airborne course, Fort Benning, Georgia; basic heavy weapons course, Fort Campbell, Kentucky; jumpmaster course, Fort Bragg, North Carolina; advance non-commissioned officer course, Fort Benning, Georgia; long range reconnaissance patrol school, Augsburg, Germany; explosive ordnance reconnaissance course, Hohenfels, Germany; counterinsurgency raider course, Fort Bragg, North Carolina; operations and intelligence course, Fort Bragg, North Carolina; special forces airborne course, Fort Bragg, North Carolina; and intelligence analyst special forces course, Fort Holabird, Maryland. By September 1968, Sergeant Bryant was serving with Company A, 5th Special Forces Group, 1st Special Forces, and was transferred to Vietnam.

Sergeant Bryant earned the Medal of Honor on March 24, 1969, at Long Khanh Province, Republic of Vietnam. His citation reads as follows:

> For conspicuous gallantry and intrepidity in action at the risk of his life above and beyond the call of duty. Sergeant First Class Bryant, assigned to Company A, distinguished himself while serving as commanding officer of Civilian Irregular Defense Group Company 321, 2d Battalion, 3d Mobile Strike Force Command, during combat operations. The battalion came under heavy fire and became surrounded by the elements of three enemy regiments. Sergeant First Class Bryant displayed extraordinary heroism throughout the succeeding 34 hours of incessant attack as he moved throughout the company position heedless of the intense hostile fire while establishing and improving the defensive perimeter, directing fire during critical phases of the battle, distributing ammunition, assisting the wounded, and providing the leadership and inspirational example of courage to his men. When a helicopter drop of ammunition was made to re-supply the beleaguered force, Sergeant First Class Bryant with complete disregard for his safety ran through the heavy enemy fire to retrieve the scattered ammunition boxes and distributed needed ammunition to his men. During a lull in the intense fighting, Sergeant First Class Bryant led a patrol outside the perimeter to obtain information of the enemy. The patrol came under intense automatic weapons fire and was pinned down. Sergeant First Class Bryant single-handedly repulsed 1 enemy attack on his small force and by his heroic action inspired his men to fight off other assaults. Seeing a wounded enemy soldier some distance from the patrol location, Sergeant First Class Bryant crawled forward alone under heavy fire to retrieve the soldier for intelligence purposes. Finding that the enemy soldier had expired, Sergeant

First Class Bryant crawled back to his patrol and led his men back to the company position where he again took command of the defense. As the siege continued, Sergeant First Class Bryant organized and led a patrol in a daring attempt to break through the enemy encirclement. The patrol had advanced some 200 meters by heavy fighting when it was pinned down by the intense automatic weapons fire from heavily fortified bunkers and Sergeant First Class Bryant was severely wounded. Despite his wounds he rallied his men, called for helicopter gunship support, and directed heavy suppressive fire upon the enemy positions. Following the last gunship attack, Sergeant First Class Bryant fearlessly charged an enemy automatic weapons position, overrunning it, and single-handedly destroying its 3 defenders. Inspired by his heroic example, his men renewed their attack on the entrenched enemy. While regrouping his small force for the final assault against the enemy, Sergeant First Class Bryant fell mortally wounded by an enemy rocket. Sergeant First Class Bryant's selfless concern for his comrades, at the cost of his life above and beyond the call of duty are in keeping with the highest traditions of the military service and reflect great credit upon himself, his unit, and the U.S. Army.

Sergeant Bryant was killed in action on March 24, 1969, at Long Khanh Province, Republic of Vietnam. President Richard M. Nixon presented the Medal of Honor to Sergeant Ashley's parents on February 16, 1971, at a ceremony at the White House.

In addition to the Medal of Honor, Sergeant Bryant also earned the Bronze Star; the Purple Heart; three Good Conduct Medals; the National Defense Service Medal; Vietnam Service Medal; Vietnam Campaign Medal (Vietnamese); the Combat Infantry Badge; and Parachutist Badge (Vietnamese).

Because he met his wife in North Carolina, William Maud Bryant was buried in the Raleigh National Cemetery, Raleigh, North Carolina. He was survived by his wife and four children.

Sergeant Rodney Maxwell Davis, USMC

5th U.S. Marines

Rodney Maxwell Davis was born on April 7, 1942, in Macon, Bibb County Georgia, the son of Gordon N. and Ruth A. Davis. On August

31, 1961, Davis enlisted in the Marine Corps at Macon, Georgia, and completed his basic training at Parris Island, South Carolina. Sergeant Davis also completed additional training at Camp Lejeune, North Carolina. In June 1961, Davis was assigned as a guard to U.S. Marine Detachment, Naval Activities, London, England. In August 1967 Davis was assigned to Company B, 1st Battalion, 5th Marines, 1st Marine Division, and sent to Vietnam.

Sergeant Davis earned the Medal of Honor on September 6, 1967, at Quang Nam Province, Republic of Vietnam. His citation reads as follows:

> For conspicuous gallantry and intrepidity at the risk of his life above and beyond the call of duty while serving as the right guide of the 2d Platoon, Company B, in action against enemy forces. Elements of the 2d Platoon were pinned down by a numerically superior force of attacking North Vietnamese Army Regulars. Remnants of the platoon were located in a trench line where Sergeant Davis was directing the fire of his men in an attempt to repel the enemy attack. Disregarding the enemy hand grenades and high volume of small arms and mortar fire, Sergeant Davis moved from man to man shouting words of encouragement to each of them while firing and throwing grenades at the onrushing enemy. When an enemy grenade landed in the trench in the midst of his men, Sergeant Davis, realizing the gravity of the situation, and in a final valiant act of complete self-sacrifice, instantly threw himself upon the grenade, absorbing with his body the full and terrific force of the explosion. Through his extraordinary initiative and inspiring valor in the face of almost certain death, Sergeant Davis saved his comrades from injury and possible loss of life, enabled his platoon to hold its vital position, and upheld the highest traditions of the Marine Corps and the U.S. Naval Service. He gallantly gave his life for his country.

Sergeant Rodney Maxwell Davis was killed in action attempting to save the men in his small command from injury or death. In recognition of his valor, Vice-President Spiro T. Agnew presented the Medal of Honor to Davis' family on March 26, 1969, at a special ceremony at the Executive Office Building in Washington, D.C.

In addition to the Medal of Honor, Sergeant Davis also earned the Purple Heart; Good Conduct Medal; National Defense Service Medal; Armed Forces Expeditionary Medal; Vietnam Service Medal: Gallantry Cross with Palm; and the Vietnam Campaign Medal (Vietnamese).

Private First Class
Robert H. Jenkins, Jr., USMC

3rd Reconnaissance Battalion

Robert Henry Jenkins, Jr., was born on June 1, 1948, at Interlachen, Putnam County, Florida, the son of Robert and Willie Mae Jenkins. On February 2, 1968, Jenkins enlisted in the U.S. Marine Corps at Jacksonville, Florida. He completed his basic training at Parris Island, South Carolina, and received additional training at Camp LeJeune, North Carolina. In July 1968, Davis was assigned to Headquarters Company, 3rd Reconnaissance Battalion, 3rd Marine Division (Rein), FMF, and transferred to Vietnam. Private Jenkins was reassigned as a machine gunner in Company C.

Private Jenkins earned the Medal of Honor on March 5, 1969, at Fire Support Base Argonne, Republic of Vietnam. His citation reads as follows:

> For conspicuous gallantry and intrepidity at the risk of his life above and beyond the call of duty while serving as a machine gunner with Company C, 3rd Reconnaissance Battalion, in connection with operations against enemy forces. Early in the morning Private First Class Jenkins' 12-man reconnaissance team was occupying a defensive position at Fire Support Base Argonne south of the Demilitarized Zone. Suddenly, the marines were assaulted by a North Vietnamese Army platoon employing mortars, automatic weapons, and hand grenades. Reacting instantly, Private First Class Jenkins and another marine quickly moved into a 2-man fighting emplacement, and as they boldly delivered accurate machine gun fire against the enemy, a North Vietnamese soldier threw a hand grenade into the emplacement. Fully realizing the inevitable results of his actions, Private First Class Jenkins quickly seized his comrade, and pushing the man to the ground, he leaped on top of the marine to shield him from the explosion. Absorbing the full impact of the detonation, Private First Class Jenkins was seriously injured and subsequently succumbed to his wounds. His courage, inspiring valor and selfless devotion to duty saved a fellow marine from serious injury or possible death and upheld the highest traditions of the Marine Corps and the U.S. Naval Service. He gallantly gave his life for his country.

Private Robert H. Jenkins was killed in action saving the life of the marine who was fighting by his side. In recognition of his valor, Vice-President Spiro T. Agnew presented the Medal of Honor to his family on April 20, 1970, at a special ceremony held at the White House. Jenkins is buried at Sister Spring Baptist Cemetery, Interlachen, Florida.

In addition to the Medal of Honor, Private Jenkins also earned the Purple Heart; National Defense Service Medal; Vietnam Service Medal with two Bronze Stars; and Vietnam Campaign Medal (Vietnamese).

Specialist Sixth Class Lawrence Joel, USA

503rd U.S. Infantry

Lawrence Joel was born on February 22, 1928, at Winston-Salem, Forsyth County, North Carolina, the son of Mr. and Mrs. Trenton Joel. Joel was raised by his foster parents, Mr. and Mrs. Clayton Samuel, of Winston-Salem, North Carolina. He graduated from the Atkins High School in Winston-Salem before joining the Army in March 1946 at New York City, New York. During his military career, Joel served in various posts in the United States, Germany, Italy, Okinawa and Vietnam. He was assigned to the Headquarters and Headquarters Company, 1st Battalion (Airborne), 503d Infantry, 173d Airborne Brigade, and in May 1965 his entire unit was sent to Vietnam.

Specialist Sixth Class Joel was the fourth soldier to earn the Medal of Honor in Vietnam. His deed of valor occurred on November 8, 1965, in Vietnam. His citation reads as follows:

> For conspicuous gallantry and intrepidity at the risk of life above and beyond the call of duty. Specialist Sixth Class Joel demonstrated indomitable courage, determination, and professional skill when a numerically superior and well-concealed Viet Cong element launched a vicious attack, which wounded or killed nearly every man in the lead squad of the company. After treating the men wounded by the initial burst of gunfire, he bravely moved forward to assist others who were wounded while proceeding to their objective. While moving from man to man, he was struck in the right leg by machine-gun fire. Although painfully wounded his desire to

aid his fellow soldiers transcended all personal feeling. He bandaged his own wound and self-administered morphine to deaden the pain, enabling him to continue his dangerous undertaking. Through this period of time, he constantly shouted words of encouragement to all around him. Then, completely ignoring the warnings of others, and his pain, he continued his search for wounded, exposing himself to hostile fire; and, as bullets dug up the dirt around him, he held plasma bottles high while kneeling, completely engrossed in his life saving mission. Then, after being struck a second time and with a bullet lodged in his thigh, he dragged himself over the battlefield and succeeded in treating 13 more men before his medical supplies ran out. Displaying resourcefulness, he saved the life of one man by placing a plastic bag over a severe chest wound to congeal the blood. As one of the platoons pursued the Viet Cong, an insurgent force in concealed positions opened fire on the platoon and wounded many more soldiers. With a new stock of medical supplies, Specialist Sixth Class Joel again shouted words of encouragement as he crawled through an intense hail of gunfire to the wounded men. After the 24-hour battle subsided and the Viet Cong dead numbered 410, snipers continued to harass the company. Throughout the long battle, Specialist Sixth Class Joel never lost sight of his mission as a medical aidman and continued to comfort and treat the wounded until his own evacuation was ordered. His meticulous attention to duty saved a large number of lives and his unselfish, daring example under most adverse conditions was an inspiration to all. Specialist Sixth Class Joel's profound concern for his fellow soldiers, at the risk of his life above and beyond the call of duty are in the highest traditions of the U.S. Army and reflect great credit upon himself and the Armed Forces of his country.

Grave of Specialist Sixth Class Lawrence Joel, USA

The Medal of Honor was presented to Specialist Sixth Class Joel by President Lyndon Johnson, on March 9, 1967, at a ceremony at the White House.

After his discharge from the Army in 1974, Joel was employed by the Veteran's Administration. Lawrence Joel died at his home in Winston-Salem, North Carolina, on February 4, 1984. His original Medal of Honor could not be located so the Army provided a replacement so that he could be buried wearing his medal. He is buried at Arlington National Cemetery, Arlington, Virginia.

Specialist Fifth Class Dwight Hal Johnson, USA

69th U.S. Armor

Dwight Hal Johnson was born out of wedlock on May 7, 1947, at Detroit, Wayne County, Michigan, the son of Mrs. Joyce Johnson Alves. Johnson for a time had a stepfather but he turned out to be an illegal alien from Jamaica and was deported. Johnson attended public schools in Detroit before he entered the service at Detroit, Michigan, on July 28, 1966. During his military career Johnson served at Fort Knox, Kentucky; the Republic of Vietnam; and Fort Carson, Colorado. Specialist Johnson was assigned to Company B, 1st Battalion, 69th Armor, 4th Infantry Division, when that unit was sent to Vietnam.

Specialist Fifth Class Dwight Johnson earned the Medal of Honor on January 15, 1968, near Dak To, Kontum Province, Republic of Vietnam. As a tank driver Johnson had served with the same tank crew since their arrival in Vietnam in February 1967. On January 14, 1967, Johnson's C.O. assigned Johnson to a different M-48 tank. The new tank's driver was sick and Johnson took the change in stride. He already had his papers for home and in another few days he would be back home.

On the morning of January 15, 1968, the four tanks of Company B, 69th Armor, sped down the road towards Dak To, when they ran straight into a NVA ambush. Without warning enemy rockets came shooting out of the jungle at the tanks and two of the tanks were hit. Hundreds of enemy soldiers came pouring out of the jungle determined to finish off their prey. Johnson watched in horror as his old tank was struck by a rocket and burst into flames. Those were Johnson's buddies and he was not going to sit and watch them burn. In a second he was out of his tank and running through a firestorm of lead towards his old tank.

Johnson had just gotten the first man out of the disabled tank, badly burned but still alive, when the tank's ammunition exploded, killing all the remainder of the crew. When the tank exploded and Johnson saw the bodies of his friends all burnt black he went berserk.

For the next 30 minutes Johnson vented his terrible rage on the North Vietnamese. Armed only with his .45 caliber pistol, with his gun blazing he ran right into the midst of the ambush killing all the NVA he could find. When his .45-caliber ran out of ammo he returned to the tank, grabbed a submachine gun and charged back into the enemy. When the machine gun ran out of ammunition he beat a North Vietnamese soldier to death with the stock of the empty weapon.

When the North Vietnamese had withdrawn he turned on the prisoners and would have killed all of them too if he had been given the chance. It took three men and three shots of morphine to hold Johnson back. Johnson was taken in a straightjacket to the hospital at Pleiku, where he lay unconscious for ten hours.

Johnson's vicious attack on the Vietnamese who had killed his buddies led to his being awarded the Medal of Honor. His citation reads as follows:

> For conspicuous gallantry and intrepidity at the risk of his life above and beyond the call of duty. Specialist Fifth Class Johnson, a tank driver with Company B, was a member of a reaction force moving to aid other elements of his platoon, which was in heavy contact with a battalion size North Vietnamese force. Specialist Fifth Class Johnson's tank, upon reaching the point of contact, threw a track and became immobilized. Realizing that he could do no more as a driver, he climbed out of the vehicle, armed only with a .45 caliber pistol. Despite intense hostile fire, Specialist Fifth Class Johnson killed several enemy soldiers before he had expended his ammunition. Returning to his tank through a heavy volume of antitank rocket, small arms and automatic weapons fire, he obtained a submachine gun with which to continue his fight against the advancing enemy. Armed with this weapon, Specialist Fifth Class Johnson again braved deadly enemy fire to return to the center of the ambush site where he courageously eliminated more of the determined foe. Engaged in extremely close combat when the last of his ammunition was expended, he killed an enemy soldier with the stock end of his submachine gun. Now weaponless, Specialist Fifth Class

Johnson ignored the enemy fire around him, climbed into his platoon sergeant's tank, extricated a wounded crew-member and carried him to an armored personnel carrier. He then returned to the same tank and assisted in firing the main gun until it jammed. In a magnificent display of courage, Specialist Fifth Class Johnson exited the tank and again armed only with a .45 caliber pistol, engaged several North Vietnamese troops in close proximity to the vehicle. Fighting his way through devastating fire and remounting his own immobilized tank, he remained fully exposed to the enemy as he bravely and skillfully engaged them with the tank's externally-mounted .50 caliber machine gun, where he remained until the situation was brought under control. Specialist Fifth Class Johnson's profound concern for his fellow soldiers, at the risk of his life above and beyond the call of duty, are in keeping with the highest traditions of the military service and reflect great credit upon himself and the U.S. Army.

Johnson was discharged from the Army in July of 1968, and he returned home to Detroit. He began to look for a job but the search proved to be futile. He visited one unemployment office after another but no one was interested in hiring a black Vietnam Vet from Detroit's worst ghetto. That all changed on November 19, 1968, when President Lyndon B. Johnson presented the Medal of Honor to Specialist Fifth Class Johnson at a ceremony at the White House. After he received the Medal of Honor suddenly all kinds of businesses that could not find work for Johnson before now had room for him in their organization.

The army also offered Johnson a job as a recruiter, which Johnson accepted. Johnson was not prepared for the celebrity and public spotlight which fell on him. He was also suffering from what we today call post-traumatic stress syndrome. Johnson began to experience financial difficulties but was too proud to ask for help. As his debts mounted so did the pressure in his life to solve this problem.

Grave of Specialist Fifth Class Dwight Hal Johnson, USA

On the dark and drizzly night of April 30, 1971, a Detroit, Michigan, liquor store clerk shot and killed a would-be robber. The dead man turned out to be an active duty Army sergeant and a recipient of the Medal of Honor, Dwight H. Johnson. Johnson is buried at Arlington National Cemetery, Arlington, Virginia.

Private First Class
Ralph H. Johnson, USMC

1st Reconnaissance Battalion

Ralph Henry Johnson was born January 11, 1949, at Charleston, Charleston County, South Carolina, the son of Mrs. Rebecca Johnson. Johnson attended public schools in Charleston before he enlisted in the Marine Corps on March 23, 1967, at Oakland, California, and was assigned to Company A, 1st Reconnaissance Battalion, 1st Marine Division (Rein), FMF. Private Johnson arrived in Vietnam on January 1, 1968.

RALPH
HENRY
JOHNSON

MEDAL OF HONOR
PFC
US MARINE CORPS
VIETNAM
JAN 11 1949
MAR 5 1968

Grave of Private First Class Ralph H. Johnson, USMC

Private Johnson earned the Medal of Honor on March 5, 1968, near the Quan Duc Valley, Republic of Vietnam. His citation reads as follows:

For conspicuous gallantry and intrepidity at the risk of his life above and beyond the call of duty while serving as a reconnaissance scout with Company A, in action against the North Vietnamese Army and Viet Cong forces. In the early morning hours during Operation ROCK, Private First Class Johnson was a member of a 15-man reconnaissance patrol manning an observation post on Hill 146 overlooking the Quan Duc Valley deep in enemy controlled territory. They were attacked by a platoon-size hostile force employing automatic weapons, satchel charges and hand grenades. Suddenly, a hand grenade landed in the three-man fighting hole occupied by Private First Class Johnson and two fellow marines. Realizing the inherent danger to his two comrades, he shouted a warning and unhesitatingly hurled himself upon the explosive device. When the grenade exploded, Private First Class Johnson absorbed the tremendous impact of the blast and was killed instantly. His prompt and heroic act saved the life of one marine at the cost of his life and undoubtedly prevented the enemy from penetrating his sector of the patrol's perimeter. Private First Class Johnson's courage, inspiring valor and selfless devotion to duty were in keeping with the highest traditions of the Marine Corps and the U.S. Naval Service. He gallantly gave his life for his country.

Private Ralph Henry Johnson was killed in action, while saving the lives of fellow marines, on March 5, 1968, at near the Quan Duc Valley, Republic of Vietnam. In recognition of his valor, Vice-President Spiro T. Agnew presented the Medal of Honor to Johnson's family on April 20, 1970, at a special ceremony at the White House. Ralph H. Johnson is buried in Beaufort National Cemetery, Beaufort, South Carolina.

Private First Class
Garfield M. Langhorn, USA

17th U.S. Cavalry

Garfield McConnell Langhorn was born on September 10, 1948, at Cumberland, Cumberland County, Virginia, the son of Garfield and Mary Langhorn. The younger Garfield Langhorn attended Riverhead High School in Riverhead, New York, where he excelled in track. He opposed the war in Vietnam, calling it senseless. Nevertheless, when he was drafted, Langhorn chose to serve his country and entered the service May 6, 1968, at Brooklyn, New York, where he was assigned to Troop C, 7th Squadron (Airmobile), 17th Cavalry, 1st Aviation Brigade. Private Langhorn served at Fort Jackson, South Carolina, and Fort Wood, Missouri, before being transferred to Vietnam.

Private Langhorn earned the Medal of Honor on January 15, 1969, at Pleiku Province, Republic of Vietnam, when he threw himself on a hand grenade to protect a group of wounded soldiers. His citation reads as follows:

> For conspicuous gallantry and intrepidity in action at the risk of his life above and beyond the call of duty. Private First Class Langhorn distinguished himself while serving as a radio operator with Troop C, near Plei Djereng in Pleiku Province. Private First Class Langhorn's platoon was inserted into a landing zone to rescue 2 pilots of a Cobra helicopter shot down by enemy fire on a heavily timbered slope. He provided radio coordination with the command-and-control aircraft overhead while the troops hacked their way through dense undergrowth to the wreckage, where both aviators were found dead. As the men were taking the bodies to a pickup site, they suddenly came under intense fire from North Vietnamese soldiers in camouflaged bunkers to the front and right flank, and within minutes they were surrounded. Private First Class Langhorn immediately radioed for help from the orbiting gunships, which began to place minigun and rocket fire on the aggressors. He then lay between the platoon leader and another man, operating the radio and providing covering fire for the wounded who had been moved to the center of the small perimeter. Darkness soon fell, making it impossible for the gunships to give accurate support, and the aggressors began to probe the perimeter. An enemy hand grenade landed in front of Private First Class Langhorn and a few feet from personnel who had become casualties. Choosing to protect these wounded, he unhesitatingly threw himself on the grenade, scooped it beneath his body and absorbed the blast. By sacrificing himself, he saved the lives of his comrades. Private First Class Langhorn's extraordinary heroism at the cost of his life was in keeping with the highest traditions of the military service and reflect great credit on himself, his unit, and the U.S. Army.

Private Garfield McConnell Langhorn was killed in action on January 15, 1969, near Plei Djereng in Pleiku Province, Republic of Vietnam. President Richard M. Nixon presented Langhorn's Medal of Honor to his family on April 7, 1970, at a ceremony at the White House. Langhorn is buried at Riverhead Cemetery, Riverhead, New York.

Sergeant Matthew Leonard

16th U.S. Infantry

Matthew Leonard was born on November 26, 1929, at Eutaw, Green County, Alabama. Leonard attended A. H. Parker High School in Birmingham, Alabama, before entering the service on August 29, 1947, at Birmingham. During his military career, Sergeant Leonard served in various locations in the United States, Japan, Korea, Germany, and Vietnam.

Sergeant Leonard was serving with Company B, 1st Battalion, 16th Infantry, 1st Infantry Division, when he earned the Medal of Honor on February 28, 1967, near Suoi Da, Republic of Vietnam. His citation reads as follows:

> For conspicuous gallantry and intrepidity in action at the risk of his life above and beyond the call of duty. His platoon was suddenly attacked by a large enemy force employing small arms, automatic weapons, and hand grenades. Although the platoon leader and several other key leaders were among the first wounded, Sergeant Leonard quickly rallied his men to throw back the initial enemy assaults. During the short pause that followed, he organized a defensive perimeter, redistributed ammunition, and inspired his comrades through his forceful leadership and words of encouragement. Noticing a wounded companion outside the perimeter, he dragged the man to safety but was struck by a sniper's bullet, which shattered his left hand. Refusing medical attention and continuously exposing himself to the increasing fire as the enemy again assaulted the perimeter, Sergeant Leonard moved from position to position to direct the fire of his men against the well camouflaged foe. Under the cover of the main attack, the enemy moved a machine gun into a location where it could sweep the entire perimeter. This threat was magnified when the platoon machine gun in this area malfunctioned. Sergeant Leonard quickly crawled to the gun position and was helping to clear the malfunction when the gunner and other men in the vicinity were wounded by fire from the enemy machine gun. Sergeant Leonard rose to his feet, charged the enemy gun and destroyed the hostile crew despite being hit several times by enemy fire. He moved to a tree, propped himself against it, and continued to engage the enemy until he succumbed to his many wounds. His fighting spirit, heroic leadership, and valiant acts inspired the

remaining members of his platoon to hold back the enemy until assistance arrived. Sergeant Leonard's profound courage and devotion to his men are in keeping with the highest traditions of the military service, and his gallant actions reflect great credit upon himself and the U.S. Army.

Sergeant Matthew Leonard was killed in action on February 28, 1967, near Suoi Da, Republic of Vietnam. Stanley R. Resor, the Secretary of the Army, presented Leonard's Medal of Honor to his family on December 19, 1968, at a ceremony at the Pentagon. Leonard is buried at Shadow Lawn Cemetery, Birmingham, Alabama.

In addition to the Medal of Honor, Sergeant Leonard also earned the Purple Heart; two Combat Infantry Badges; three Good Conduct Medals; Army of Occupation Medal with Japan and Germany clasps; Korean Service Medal with four Bronze Service Stars; National Defense Service Medal; Vietnam Service Medal; Military Merit Medal (Vietnamese); Victoria Campaign Medal (Vietnamese); and the United Nations Service Medal.

Sergeant Donald Russell Long, USA

4th U.S. Cavalry

Donald Russell Long was born on August 27, 1939, at Blackfork, Ohio, the son of Mr. and Mrs. Herman Long. Long was drafted into the Army on April 16, 1963, at Ashland, Kentucky. In September 1965, he was assigned to Troop C, 1st Squadron, 4th Cavalry, 1st Infantry Division, at Fort Riley, Kansas. His entire unit was then transferred to Vietnam.

Sergeant Long earned the Medal of Honor on June 30, 1966, in Vietnam. His citation reads as follows:

> For conspicuous gallantry and intrepidity in action at the risk of his life above and beyond the call of duty. Troops B and C, while conducting a reconnaissance mission along a road, were suddenly attacked by a Viet Cong regiment, supported by mortars, recoilless rifles and machine guns, from concealed positions astride the road. Sergeant Long abandoned the relative safety of his armored personnel carrier and braved a withering hail of enemy fire to carry wounded men to evacuation helicopters. As the platoon fought its way

forward to re-supply advanced elements, Sergeant Long repeatedly exposed himself to enemy fire at point blank range to provide the needed supplies. While assaulting the Viet Cong position, Sergeant Long inspired his comrades by fearlessly standing unprotected to repel the enemy with rifle fire and grenades as they attempted to mount his carrier. When the enemy threatened to overrun a disabled carrier nearby, Sergeant Long again disregarded his own safety to help the severely wounded crew to safety. As he was handing arms to the less seriously wounded and reorganizing them to press the attack, an enemy grenade was hurled onto the carrier deck. Immediately recognizing the imminent danger, he instinctively shouted a warning to the crew and pushed to safety one man who had not heard his warning over the roar of battle. Realizing that these actions would not fully protect the exposed crewmen from the deadly explosion, he threw himself over the grenade to absorb the blast and thereby saved the lives of 8 of his comrades at the expense of his life. Throughout the battle, Sergeant Long's extraordinary heroism, courage and supreme devotion to his men were in the finest tradition of the military service, and reflect great credit upon himself and the U.S. Army.

Sergeant Donald Russell Long gave his life for his country on June 30, 1966, in Vietnam. Secretary of the Army Stanley R. Resor presented the Medal of Honor to Long's family on February 8, 1968, at a ceremony at the Pentagon. Long is buried the Union Baptist Church Cemetery, Blackfork, Ohio.

In addition to his Medal of Honor, Sergeant Long also earned the following awards and decorations: Purple Heart; Good Conduct Medal; National Defense Service Medal; Vietnam Service Medal with Bronze Service Star; Vietnam Campaign Medal (Vietnamese); and Combat Infantry Badge.

Private First Class
Milton L. Olive, III, USA

503rd U.S. Infantry

Milton Lee Olive, III, was born on November 7, 1946, at Chicago, Cook County, Illinois, the son of Milton L. Olive, Jr., and Clair Lee Olive.

Milton Olive attended Saints Junior College High School in Chicago before he quit school in his junior year. On August 17, 1964, he enlisted in the U.S. Army at Chicago. In May 1969 Private Olive was assigned to Company B, 2d Battalion (Airborne), 503rd Infantry, 173d Airborne Brigade.

Private Olive was the first African American to earn the Medal of Honor in Vietnam. His deed of valor occurred on October 22, 1965, at Phu Cuong, Republic of Vietnam. His citation reads as follows:

> For conspicuous gallantry and intrepidity at the risk of his life above and beyond the call of duty. Private First Class Olive was a member of the 3d Platoon of Company B, as it moved through the jungle to find the Viet Cong operating in the area. Although the platoon was subjected to a heavy volume of enemy gunfire and pinned down temporarily, it retaliated by assaulting the Viet Cong positions, causing the enemy to flee. As the platoon pursued the insurgents, Private First Class Olive and four other soldiers were moving through the jungle together a grenade was thrown into their midst. Private First Class Olive saw the grenade, and then saved the lives of his fellow soldiers at the sacrifice of his by grabbing the grenade in his hand and falling on it to absorb the blast with his body. Through his bravery, unhesitating actions, and complete disregard for his safety, he prevented additional loss of life or injury to the members of his platoon. Private First Class Olive's extraordinary heroism at the risk of his life above and beyond the call of duty was in the highest tradition of the U.S. Army and reflects great credit upon himself and the Armed Forces of his country.

Private Milton Lee Olive gallantly gave his life for his country on October 22, 1965, at Phu Cuong, Republic of Vietnam. In recognition of his valor, President Lyndon B. Johnson presented the Medal of Honor to his family on April 26, 1966, at a ceremony at the White House. The ceremony was attended by Lieutenant James Sanford and Specialist 4th Class John Foster, two of the men whom Olive had saved. Chicago Mayor Richard Daly was also present. President Johnson in his remarks said, "Words can never enlarge upon acts of heroism and duty, but this nation will never forget Milton Lee Olive."

Milton L. Olive is buried at West Grove Cemetery, Lexington, Mississippi.

In addition to his Medal of Honor, Milton Olive also earned the following awards and decorations: Purple Heart with Oak Leaf Cluster; Armed Forces Expeditionary Medal; and Combat Infantryman Badge.

Captain Riley L. Pitts, USA

27th U.S. Infantry

Riley Leroy Pitts was born on October 15, 1937, at Fallis, Oklahoma, the son of Mr. and Mrs. Theodore H. Pitts. Riley attended the University of Wichita before he entered the Army on June 5, 1960, at Wichita, Kansas. On December 1966, Captain Pitts was assigned to serve as commander of Company C, 2d Battalion, 27th Infantry, 25th Infantry Division.

Captain Pitts earned the Medal of Honor on October 31, 1967, at Ap Dong, Republic of Vietnam. His citation reads as follows:

> Distinguishing himself by exceptional heroism while serving as company commander during an airmobile assault. Immediately after his company landed in the area, several Viet Cong opened fire with automatic weapons. Despite the enemy fire, Captain Pitts forcefully led an assault, which overran the enemy positions. Shortly thereafter, Captain Pitts was ordered to move his unit to the north to reinforce another company heavily engaged against a strong enemy force. As Captain Pitts' company moved forward to engage the enemy, intense fire was received from three directions, including fire from four enemy bunkers, two of which were within 15 meters of Capt. Pitts' position. The severity of the incoming fire prevented Captain Pitts from maneuvering his company. His rifle fire proving ineffective against the enemy due to the dense jungle foliage, he picked up an M-79 grenade launcher and began pinpointing the targets. Seizing a Chinese Communist grenade, which had been taken from a captured Viet Cong's web gear, Captain Pitts lobbed the grenade at a bunker to his front, but it hit the dense jungle foliage and rebounded. Without hesitation, Captain Pitts threw himself on top of the grenade, which, fortunately, failed to explode. Captain Pitts then directed the repositioning of the company to permit friendly artillery to be fired. Upon completion of the artillery fire mission, Captain Pitts again led his men toward the enemy positions, personally killing at least one more Viet Cong. The jungle growth still prevented effective fire to be placed on the enemy bunkers. Captain Pitts, displaying complete disregard for his life and personal safety, quickly moved to a position, which permitted him to place effective fire on the enemy. He maintained a continuous fire, pinpointing the enemy's fortified positions, while at the same time directing and urging his men forward, until he was mortally wounded.

Captain Pitts' conspicuous gallantry, extraordinary heroism, and intrepidity at the cost of his life, above and beyond the call of duty, are in the highest traditions of the U.S. Army and reflect great credit upon himself, his unit, and the Armed Forces of his country.

Captain Riley Leroy Pitts was killed in action, leading his company against the Viet Cong on October 31, 1967, at Ap Dong, Republic of Vietnam. In recognition of his valor, President Lyndon B. Johnson presented the Medal of Honor to his family on December 10, 1968, at a ceremony at the White House. Riley L. Pitts is buried at Hillcrest Memorial Gardens Cemetery, Spencer, Oklahoma.

In addition to the Medal of Honor, Captain Pitts earned the following awards and decorations: Silver Star Medal; Bronze Star Medal; Purple Heart; Combat Infantry Badge; National Defense Service Medal; Meritorious Unit Citation; Parachutist Badge; Expert Infantryman Badge; National Order of Vietnam (Vietnamese); Gallantry Cross with Palm (Vietnamese) and the Vietnam Campaign Medal.

Lieutenant-Colonel Charles Calvin Rogers, USA

5th U.S. Artillery

Charles Calvin Rogers was born on September 6, 1929, at Claremont, West Virginia, the son of Mr. and Mrs. Clyde Rogers, Sr., of Indianapolis, Indiana. Charles Rogers graduated from West Virginia State College with a degree in mathematics. He wanted to be a minister.

Rogers enlisted in the Army at Institute, West Virginia, and was eventually made lieutenant-colonel of 1st Battalion, 5th Artillery, 1st Infantry Division. During his military career, Lieutenant-Colonel Rogers was stationed at various posts in the United States, Germany, Korea and Vietnam.

Lieutenant-Colonel Rogers is the highest-ranking African American to earn the Medal of Honor. His deed of valor occurred on November 1, 1968, at the Fishhook, near the Cambodian border, Republic of Vietnam. His citation reads as follows:

For conspicuous gallantry and intrepidity in action at the risk of his life above and beyond the call of duty. Lieutenant Colonel Rogers, Field Artillery, distinguished himself in action while serving as commanding officer, 1st Battalion, during the defense of a forward fire support base. In the early morning hours, the fire support base was subjected to a concentrated bombardment of heavy mortar, rocket and rocket propelled grenade fire. Simultaneously the position was struck by a human wave ground assault, led by sappers who breached the defensive barriers with bangalore torpedoes and penetrated the defensive perimeter. Lieutenant Colonel Rogers with complete disregard for his safety moved through the hail of fragments from bursting enemy rounds to the embattled area. He aggressively rallied the dazed artillery crewmen to man their howitzers and he directed their fire on the assaulting enemy. Although knocked to the ground and wounded by an exploding round, Lieutenant Colonel Rogers sprang to his feet and led a small counterattack force against an enemy element that had penetrated the howitzer positions. Although painfully wounded a second time during the assault, Lieutenant Colonel Rogers pressed the attack killing several of the enemy and driving the remainder from the positions. Refusing medical treatment, Lieutenant Colonel Rogers reestablished and reinforced the defensive positions. As a second human wave attack was launched against another sector of the perimeter, Lieutenant Colonel Rogers directed artillery fire on the assaulting enemy and led a second counterattack against the charging forces. His valorous example rallied the beleaguered defenders to repulse and defeat the enemy onslaught. Lieutenant Colonel Rogers moved from position to position through the heavy enemy fire, giving encouragement and direction to his men. At dawn the determined enemy launched a third assault against the fire-base in an attempt to overrun the position. Lieutenant Colonel Rogers moved to the threatened area and directed lethal fire on the enemy forces. Seeing a howitzer inoperative due to casualties, Lieutenant Colonel Rogers joined the surviving members of the crew to return the howitzer to action. While directing the position defense, Lieutenant Colonel Rogers was seriously wounded by fragments from a heavy mortar round which exploded on the parapet of the gun position. Although too severely wounded to physically lead the defenders, Lieutenant Colonel Rogers continued to give encouragement and direction to his men in the defeating and repelling of the enemy attack. Lieutenant Colonel Rogers' dauntless courage and heroism inspired the defenders of the fire support base to the heights of valor to defeat a determined and numerically superior enemy force. His relentless spirit of aggressiveness in action is in the highest tradition of the

military service and reflects great credit upon himself, his
unit, and the U.S. Army.

President Richard M. Nixon, in recognition of conspicuous gallantry, above and beyond the call of duty, awarded the Medal of Honor
to Lieutenant-Colonel Charles C. Rogers on May 14, 1970, at a ceremony
at the White House.

Lieutenant-Colonel Charles Calvin Rogers, USA, and his grave.

In addition to the Medal of Honor, Lieutenant-Colonel Rogers earned
the Legion of Merit; Distinguished Flying Cross; Bronze Star with V device;
Air Medal with nine Oak Leaf Clusters; Joint Service Commendation
Medal; Army Commendation Medal with two Oak Leaf Clusters; Purple
Heart; National Defense Service Medal with one Oak Leaf Cluster; Army
of Occupation (Germany); Parachutist Badge; Vietnam Service Medal
(Vietnamese); and the Vietnam Campaign Medal (Vietnamese).

Rogers retired from the service as a major general on January 1, 1984.
He then went on to fulfill his other dream and was ordained a Baptist
minister. His parish consisted of the young American soldiers stationed
in Europe. Charles Calvin Rogers died of cancer on September 21, 1990,
at his home in Munich, Germany. Rogers was cremated and his ashes
interred at Arlington National Cemetery, Arlington, Virginia.

1st Lieutenant Ruppert L. Sargent, USA

9th U.S. Infantry

Ruppert Leon Sargent was born January 6, 1938, at Hampton, Hampton County, Virginia. Sargent attended Virginia State College and the Hampton Institute before enlisting in the Army on January 8, 1959, at Richmond, Virginia. Although raised a Jehovah's Witness, Sargent's attraction to the military overcame his religious beliefs. After six years as an enlisted man Sargent was accepted at Officer Training School. He received the gold bars of a lieutenant on October 15, 1965. In 1966, Lieutenant Sargent was assigned to Vietnam for duty with Company B, 4th Battalion, 9th Infantry, 25th Infantry Division.

Lieutenant Sargent earned the Medal of Honor on March 15, 1967, at Hau Nghia Province, Republic of Vietnam. His citation reads as follows:

> For conspicuous gallantry and intrepidity in action at the risk of his life above and beyond the call of duty. While leading a platoon of Company B, First Lieutenant Sargent was investigating a reported Viet Cong meeting house and weapons cache. A tunnel entrance which First Lieutenant Sargent observed was booby trapped. He tried to destroy the booby trap and blow the cover from the tunnel using hand grenades, but this attempt was not successful. He and his demolition man moved in to destroy the booby trap and cover which flushed a Viet Cong soldier from the tunnel, who was immediately killed by the nearby platoon sergeant. First Lieutenant Sargent, the platoon sergeant, and a forward observer moved toward the tunnel entrance. As they approached, another Viet Cong emerged and threw two hand grenades that landed in the midst of the group. First Lieutenant Sargent fired three shots at the enemy, then turned and unhesitatingly threw himself over the two grenades. He was mortally wounded, and his two companions were lightly wounded when the grenades exploded. By his courageous and selfless act of exceptional heroism, he saved the lives of the platoon sergeant and forward observer and prevented the injury or death of several other nearby comrades. First Lieutenant Sargent's actions were in keeping with the highest traditions of the military services and reflect great credit upon himself and the U.S. Army.

Lieutenant Ruppert Leon Sargent valiantly gave his life for his country on March 15, 1967, at Hau Nghia Province, Republic of Vietnam. In

July 1968 the recommendation for Sargent's posthumous Medal of Honor was approved, making him the first black officer so honored.

Much to their shock and surprise, when Pentagon officials contacted Sargent's widow to arrange for the presentation ceremony, she refused to accept the award. Her position stemmed from her strong religious beliefs. A Jehovah's Witness professes allegiance to God alone and not to any organized government. Sargent's mother, also a Jehovah's Witness, supported her daughter-in-law's position. Both women had opposed Sargent's enlistment into the Army.

For months pentagon officials worked through quiet diplomacy with Mrs. Sargent and she finally agreed to accept the award provided that it was awarded in a private ceremony with no publicity. In recognition of Sargent's sacrifices above and beyond the call of duty, on March 7, 1969, General Donley P. Bolton presented the Medal of Honor to Lieutenant Sargent's widow at her home in Hampton, Virginia. Ruppert Sargent is buried in Hampton National Cemetery, Hampton, Virginia.

Specialist 5th Class Clarence Eugene Sasser, USA

60th U.S. Infantry

Specialist 5th Class Clarence Eugene Sasser, USA

Clarence Eugene Sasser was born on September 12, 1947, at Chenango, Texas. Sasser wanted to become a doctor and was attending the University of Houston when he was drafted into the Army on June 15, 1967, at Houston, Texas. By 1968, Specialist 5th Class Sasser had been transferred to Vietnam as part of the Headquarters Company, 3d Battalion, 60th Infantry, 9th Infantry Division.

During his military career Specialist 5th Class Sasser earned the Medal of Honor; Purple Heart; Combat Medical Badge; National Service Medal; and Vietnam Campaign Medal (Vietnamese).

Specialist Five Sasser earned the Medal of Honor on January 10, 1968, at Ding Tuong Province, Republic of Vietnam. His citation reads as follows:

> For conspicuous gallantry and intrepidity in action at the risk of his life above and beyond the call of duty. Specialist Fifth Class Sasser distinguished himself while assigned to Headquarters and Headquarters Company, 3d Battalion. He was serving as a medical aidman with Company A, 3d Battalion, on a reconnaissance in force operation. His company was making an air assault when suddenly it was taken under heavy small arms, recoilless rifle, machine-gun and rocket fire from well fortified enemy positions on three sides of the landing zone. During the first few minutes, over 30 casualties were sustained. Without hesitation, Specialist Fifth Class Sasser ran across an open rice paddy through a hail of fire to assist the wounded. After helping one man to safety, he was painfully wounded in the left shoulder by fragments of an exploding rocket. Refusing medical attention, he ran through a barrage of rocket and automatic weapons fire to aid casualties of the initial attack and, after giving them urgently needed treatment, continued to search for other wounded. Despite two additional wounds immobilizing his legs, he dragged himself through the mud toward another soldier 100 meters away. Although in agonizing pain and faint from loss of blood, Specialist Fifth Class Sasser reached the man, treated him, and proceeded on to encourage another group of soldiers to crawl 200 meters to relative safety. There he attended their wounds for 5 hours until they were evacuated. Specialist Fifth Class Sasser's extraordinary heroism is in keeping with the highest traditions of the military service and reflects great credit upon himself, his unit, and the U.S. Army.

For his extraordinary courage, President Richard M. Nixon awarded Specialist Fifth Class Sasser the Medal of Honor on March 7, 1969, at a special ceremony at the White House.

After the his discharge, Clarence Sasser attended Texas A&M University, where he had been offered a scholarship. He then worked for six years for a chemical company and now works for the Veterans Administration. In 1971, Sasser married his wife Ethel, and he has two sons.

Sergeant Clifford Chester Sims, USA

501st U.S. Infantry

Clifford Chester Sims was born on June 18, 1942, at Port St. Joe, Gulf County, Florida. Sims entered the service at Jacksonville, Florida, and was assigned to U.S. Army, Company D, 2d Battalion (Airborne), 501st Infantry, 101st Airborne Division.

Sergeant Sims earned the Medal of Honor on February 21, 1968, near Hue, Republic of Vietnam. His citation reads as follows:

> For conspicuous gallantry and intrepidity in action at the risk of his life above and beyond the call of duty. Staff Sergeant Sims distinguished himself while serving as a squad leader with Company D. Company D was assaulting a heavily fortified enemy position concealed within a dense wooded area when it encountered strong enemy defensive fire. Once within the wood-line, Staff Sergeant Sims led his squad in a furious attack against an enemy force which had pinned down the 1st Platoon and threatened to overrun it. His skillful leadership provided the platoon with freedom of movement and enabled it to regain the initiative. Staff Sergeant Sims was then ordered to move his squad to a position where he could provide covering fire for the company command group and to link up with the 3d Platoon, which was under heavy enemy pressure. After moving no more than 30 meters Staff Sergeant Sims noticed that a brick structure in which ammunition was stocked was on fire. Realizing the danger, Staff Sergeant Sims took immediate action to move his squad from this position. Though in the process of leaving the area two members of his squad were injured by the subsequent explosion of the ammunition, Staff Sergeant Sims' prompt actions undoubtedly prevented more serious casualties from occurring. While continuing through the dense woods amidst heavy enemy fire, Staff Sergeant Sims and his squad were approaching a bunker when they heard the unmistakable noise of a concealed booby trap being triggered immediately to their front. Staff Sergeant Sims warned his comrades of the danger and unhesitatingly hurled himself upon the device as it exploded, taking the full impact of the blast. In so protecting his fellow soldiers, he willingly sacrificed his life. Staff Sergeant Sims' extraordinary heroism at the cost of his life is in keeping with the highest traditions of the military service and reflects great credit upon himself and the U.S. Army.

Staff Sergeant Clifford Chester Sims gave his life to save his comrades on February 21, 1968, near Hue, Republic of Vietnam. In recognition of his conspicuous gallantry, Vice-President Spiro T. Agnew presented the Medal of Honor to Sims' family on December 2, 1969. Sims is buried in Barrancas National Cemetery, Pensacola, Florida.

1st Lieutenant John Earl Warren, USA

22nd U.S. Infantry

John Earl Warren was born on November 16, 1946, at Brooklyn, Kings County, New York. Warren enlisted in the Army at New York City, New York, and was eventually promoted to first lieutenant and assigned to Company C, 2d Battalion (Mechanized), 22d Infantry, 25th Infantry Division.

Lieutenant Warren earned the Medal of Honor on January 14, 1969, at Tay Ninh Province, Republic of Vietnam. His citation reads as follows:

For conspicuous gallantry and intrepidity in action at the risk of his life above and beyond the call of duty. First Lieutenant Warren distinguished himself at the cost of his life while serving as a platoon leader with Company C. While moving through a rubber plantation to reinforce another friendly unit, Company C came under intense fire from a well-fortified enemy force. Disregarding his safety, First Lieutenant Warren with several of his men began maneuvering through the hail of enemy fire toward the hostile positions. When he had come to within six feet of one of the enemy

1st Lieutenant John E. Warren, USA

bunkers and was preparing to toss a hand grenade into it, an enemy grenade was suddenly thrown into the middle of his small group. Thinking only of his men, First Lieutenant Warren fell in the direction of the grenade, thus shielding those around him from the blast. His action, performed at the cost of his life, saved three men from serious or mortal injury. First Lieutenant Warren's ultimate action of sacrifice to save the lives of his men was in keeping with the highest traditions of the military service and reflects great credit on him, his unit, and the U.S. Army.

Lieutenant John Earl Warren gave his life in the service of his country on January 14, 1969, at Tay Ninh Province, Republic of Vietnam. In recognition of his valor above and beyond the call of duty, President Richard M. Nixon presented the Medal of Honor to his family on August 6, 1970, at a special ceremony at the White House. Warren is buried at Long Island National Cemetery, Farmingdale, New York.

Appendix

Number of Medals of Honor Awarded, by Wars and Campaigns

Medal of Honor statistics can often be confusing and even contradictory, especially if you take information from a variety of published or Internet sources. However, well researched material is not contradictory, even when the numbers differ from source to source. Consider the following:

Since it was established in 1861 a total of 3,458 Medals of Honor (Army, Navy/Marine Corps, and Air Force) have been awarded for specific acts of heroism. During World War I, however, five marines received both the Army Medal of Honor and the Navy Medal of Honor for the same action. This means that there have actually been 3,453 separate acts of valor that have been recognized with the award of a Medal of Honor.

Of the 3,453 heroic actions, 14 were performed by men who had previously been awarded Medals of Honor for a different action (these 14 plus the 5 World War I Marines comprise the 19 *double awardees* of the Medal of Honor). When these 14 second actions by a previous Medal of Honor recipient are subtracted from the total number of Medal of Honor actions, the total number of individuals who have earned the Medal of Honor is 3,439.

Of the 3,439 individuals who have received Medals of Honor, five were awarded to foreign nationals (the unknown soldiers of Belgium, Great Britain, France, Italy, and Rumania).

KEY: A: Army. N: Navy. MC: Marine Corps. AAC: Army
Air Corps. CG: Coast Guard. AF: Air Force.

	Total	A	N	MC	AAC	CG	AF
Civil War	1522	1198	307	17			
Indian Wars	426	426					
Korea 1871	15		9	6			
Spanish-American War	110	31	64	15			
Samoa	4		1	3			
Philippine Insurection	80	69	5	6			
Philippine Outlaws	6	1	5				
China (Boxer Rebellion)	59	4	22	33			
Mexico (Vera Cruz)	56	1	46	9			
Haiti 1915	6			6			
Dominican Republic	3			3			
World War I	119	86	21	8	4		
Haiti 1919-1920	2			2			
Nicaraguan Campaign	2			2			
World War II	464	287	57	82	37	1	
Korean War	131	78	7	42			4
Vietnam War	244	158	16	57			13
Somalia	2	2					
Peacetime	193	2	185	5	1		
Unknown Soldiers	9	9					

Bibliography

Books

Amos, Preston. *Above and Beyond in the West: Black Medal of Honor Winners, 1870–1890.* Washington DC: Potomac Corral, 1974.

Beyer, W. F., and O.F. Keyel, eds. *Deeds of Valor.* 2 vols. Detroit: Perrien-Keydel, 1906–7.

Blair, Clay. *The Forgotten War: America In Korea.* New York: Times Books, 1987.

Greene, Robert E. *Black Defenders of America, 1775–1973.* Chicago: Johnson, 1974.

Hardy, Gordon, ed. *Above and Beyond.* Boston: Boston Publishing, 1985.

Jones, W. J., ed. *The Story of American Heroism.* Springfield, IL: The Werner Company, 1896.

Katz, William L. *Black Indians: A Hidden Heritage.* New York: Atheneum Books, 1986.

Kayser, Hugh. *The Spirit of America: The Biographies of Forty Living Congressional Medal of Honor Recipients.* Palm Springs, CA: ETC Publications, 1982.

Kennedy, Francis H., ed. *The Civil War Battlefield Guide.* Arlington: The Conservative Fund, 1990.

Lang, George, Raymond L. Collins, and Gerard White. *Medal of Honor Recipients 1863–1994.* New York: Facts on File, 1995.

Leckie, William H. *The Buffalo Soldiers: A Narrative of the Negro Cavalry in the West.* Norman: University of Oklahoma Press, 1967.

Lee, Irvin H. *Negro Medal of Honor Men.* New York: Dodd, Mead, 1967.

Lowery, Timothy S. *And Brave Men, Too.* New York: Berkley Books, 1985.

_____. *Valor.* New York: Berkley Books, 1989.

Mitchell, Joseph B. *The Badge of Gallantry.* New York: The Macmillan Company, 1968.

Murphy, Edward F. *Korean War Heroes.* Navado: Presidio Press, 1992.

_____. *Vietnam Medal of Honor Heroes.* New York: Ballantine Books, 1987.

Peterson, Howard. *Stand Silent.* New York: Vantage Press, 1975.

Reedstrom, E. Lisle. *Apache Wars: An Illustrated Battle History.* New York: Sterling, 1990.

Schubert, Frank N. *Black Valor: Buffalo Sol-diers and the Medal of Honor 1870–1898.* Wilmington: Scholarly Resources Inc., 1997.

Tassin, R. *Double Winners of the Medal of Honor.* Canton, Ohio: Daring Books, 1987.

Trapp, Dan L., ed. *Encyclopedia of Frontier Biography.* Lincoln: University of Nebraska Press, 1988.

Articles

Aliyetti, John E. "Gallantry Under Fire." *Civil War Times Illustrated,* October 1996 p.50.

Amos, Preston. "'Augustus Walley Day' Observed in Maryland County." *The Annals.* Vol. 17:1, p.11.

Amos Preston. "Black Heroes Honored." *The Annals.* Vol. 7:2, p.33.

_____. "Buffalo Soldier Found." *The Annals.* Vol. 16:3, p.57.

_____. "Facts About the Birth Place of Robert Blake, USN Civil War." *The Annals.* Vol. 1:1, p.5.

_____. "Ship Named for Black Marine Hero." *The Annals.* Vol. 10:1, p.21.

Bozich, Stan. "William M. Bryant." *The Annals.* Vol. 12:4, p.82.

Collins, Raymond L. "The Facts About Robert A. Sweeney." *The Annals.* Vol. 9:2, p.32.

_____. "Ralph H. Johnson." *The Annals.* Vol. 12:4, p.80.

_____. "78th Black Medal of Honor Hero Found." *The Annals.* Vol. 10:2, p.33.

Cranefield, Ben, Jr. "Milton Lee Olive — An American Hero." *The Annals.* Vol. 13:3, p.59.

Galloway, Joseph L. "Debt of Honor." *U.S. News & World Report.* Vol. 120:18, p.28.

Hanna, Charles W. "Dwight H. Johnson." *The Annals.* Vol. 22:3, p.81.

_____. "Sergeant Moses Williams and Private Augustus Walley." *The Annals.* Vol. 20:1, p.8.

Impoco, Jim. "The War Hero from the Back of the Bus." *U.S. News & World Report.* Vol. 120:18, p.41.

Kenney, Jim. "Four 'Lost' Heroes Honored." *The Annals.* Vol. 11:3, p.55.

Langellier, John. "Between 1865 and 1890, 18 buffalo soldiers Won the Medal of Honor in the American West." *Military History.* Vol. 13:6, p.16.

Levstik, Frank R. "From Slavery to Freedom." *Civil War Times Illustrated.* November 1972, p.10.

Moore, Gayla R. "Vietnam Hero Remembered." *The Annals.* Vol.12:3, p.64.

Murphy, Edward F. "Seven African-Americans Honored." *The Annals.* Vol. 18:3, p.43.

_____. "Seven African-Americans Up for Medal of Honor." *The Annals.* Vol.17:4, p.67.

_____. "World War I Medal of Honor Awarded." *The Annals.* Vol. 13:4, p.75.

Reichley, John. "Buffalo Soldier Honored." *The Annals.* Vol. 13:1, p.10.
Smith, Stan. "Five Medal of Honor Heroes Buried in Small Town." *The Annals.* Vol. 9:4, p.93.
Tinklepaugh, Clyde. "African-American Vietnam Hero Remembered." *The Annals.* Vol. 15:2, p.35.
Urwin, Gregory J.W. "I Want You to Prove Yourselves Men." *Civil War Times Illustrated,* December 1989, p.42.
VanKluyve, John. "George Henry Wanton — Black Hero of Tayabacca, Cuba." *The Annals.* Vol. 4:3, p.53.
Wharfield, H. B. "Army Issues Official Apology to Wronged World War II Medal of Honor Winner." *Jet Magazine.* November 29, 1999.
_____. "Clarence E. Sasser — First Black Texan To Earn Medal of Honor." *The Annals.* Vol. 2:3, p.61.
_____. "Decatur Dorsey." *The Annals.* Vol. 7:2, p.34.
_____. "Lawrence Joel." *The Annals.* Vol. 6:3, p.42.

Website

Medal of Honor Recipients Buried in Arlington National Cemetery http://www.arlingtoncemetery.com/medalofh.htm

Index